C000132205

Expressions of Faith
Ulster's Church Heritage

Richard Oram

Colourpoint

All rights reserved. No part of this publication may be reproduced, stored in a retrieval system or transmitted in any form or by any means, electronic, mechanical, photocopying, scanning, recording or otherwise, without the prior written permission of the copyright owners and publisher of this book.

6 5 4 3 2 1

© Richard Oram
  Newtownards 2001

Designed by Colourpoint Books, Newtownards
Printed by Nicholson and Bass Ltd

ISBN 1 898392 74 9

Colourpoint Books
Unit D5, Ards Business Centre
Jubilee Road
NEWTOWNARDS
County Down
Northern Ireland
BT23 4YH
Tel: 028 9182 0505
Fax: 028 9182 1900
E-mail: info@colourpoint.co.uk
Web-site: www.colourpoint.co.uk

About the Author

Dick Oram is a freelance consultant architect specialising in building conservation. Born in Oxford in 1938, he attended the Cathedral School and then studied at the Architectural Association in London.

His connection with Northern Ireland began in 1967 when he became involved with the development of the new city of Craigavon. This work led to the creation of a close bond with the Ulster Architectural Heritage Society.

The past two decades have been spent with the DOE (NI) Historic Buildings Branch (now the Environment and Heritage Service), where churches have been a particular subject of study.

All photographs in the book are by the author, unless otherwise stated.

Cover Photographs

Front:
  Middle Church of Ireland, Ballinderry

Rear:
  top left – St Patrick's Roman Catholic Church, Dungannon
  top right – St Patrick's Church of Ireland, Jordanstown
  bottom left – Apsley Hall, Donegall Pass, Belfast
  bottom right – St John's Church of Ireland, Clondehorky, Co Donegal

ACKNOWLEDGMENTS

Working on this short book has been a fascinating experience. I have learnt a great deal in the process. A great debt is due to the cooperation of the many priests, ministers, committee members etc who have freely and patiently given of their time at each building that I have visited. Thanks are due to the library staff of the South Eastern Education and Library Board, who have supplied me with some fairly obscure reading and reference material. My special thanks goes to Gail Pollock who, in her holidays, took a great many of the photographs that illustrate this work; and to Sheila McEvoy, who has learnt to read my writing and has carried out all the word processing.

Contents

Contents

Introduction

Church buildings form one of the most striking elements of our built heritage. They are generally prominently sited in both urban and rural settings. Where they feature steeples or towers these are critical elements in the landscape, often visible for miles around, forming the skyline of many of our major towns and villages. It is only in very recent times that commercial and manufacturing developments have overtaken churches, to become the most conspicuous contributors to the built environment. We have become so used to their presence that we may take them for granted, yet, increasingly, they are coming under threat. Two major factors in this development are population migration and the growing materialistic outlook of western society. The place of the church in our culture is no longer as secure as it was, making this an appropriate time to survey this treasury and take stock of its values.

In structuring this book, I have first sketched the context in which the building forms have been derived and then outlined the developments of style and function, through time, and in the context of denominational differences. The focus of the book is on buildings in use, but a short note on historical development is included.

The written work has been supplemented by visits to a limited number of sites and these are illustrated and explained in brief written commentaries. The selection of these sites has been the most difficult part of the whole exercise, and what has been included and what left out will in all probability draw the most criticism. Only one cathedral has been included, and that is because it is the only medieval building in Northern Ireland to have remained in regular use for Christian worship and to have retained its medieval appearance very much intact. This building is of course the old cathedral in Armagh, but, taken as a group, cathedrals are special in so many ways that they do not compare directly with church buildings erected for everyday congregational worship. Hence, with this one exception, I have otherwise left them out of this study.

The criteria applied in the final selection of sites included age, geographical spread, architectural style and denomination. The richness in history, culture and architectural diversity, even within these few examples, will, I hope, stir readers to go out and to look at the many other important ecclesiastical buildings around them.

Not only are there many more buildings left to investigate, there are also other aspects of interest to be discovered, in and around each one. These I have not had time to elaborate on at all – for example, bells, organs, glass, monuments, clocks, sundials, symbolism, furnishing – and so you can go on, the list is immense. While some buildings certainly hold more in store than others, there is no such place as a boring church. A great many of these buildings have been researched by local historians. Their findings have often been made available to me in my journeying and these studies certainly are a mine of information. If you live somewhere that does not yet have a written history, think seriously about tackling this job yourself. All you need is time and patience. There is no doubt that you will find the work extremely rewarding. A surprising number of churches' officials have no idea what documents they possess. Plans, accounts, minute books, registers and the like are, historically speaking, extremely valuable, and simply to index them and store them safely in some sort of order is very worthwhile work. If you would like guidance for such an undertaking it would be well worth your while to contact the Ulster Historic Churches Trust.

The Development of Church Buildings in Ulster

The Early and Medieval Church

In the early days of Christianity, worshippers met in each others houses and outhouses. This was probably the case with Christian beginnings in Ireland, when in the fifth century the first missionaries came to these shores. However, by that time the idea of constructing a building specifically for Christian worship was already well established in mainland Europe. Considering the unsettled nature of early Irish history, it may be surprising to see the number of very early ecclesiastical buildings and monuments that survive today, albeit in a ruinous state. Dr Hamlin has remarked too, that in Ireland, by comparison with other countries, many of these remains can still be viewed in the landscape context in which they were first built, since here the march of time has not so often brought about the same degree of change in the landscape, as is experienced elsewhere in the western world.

Christian culture in Ireland flourished and developed for four centuries before the Vikings began to arrive in serious numbers. The evidence we have of these early buildings is that they were extremely simple, rectangular structures, almost without architectural pretension. Common features were a west door and an east window. The remains now surviving are of stone-built buildings, but there must have been many more of timber and earth construction, of which there is absolutely no record. The close of this first chapter of church development is the age of round towers and high crosses, generally associated with monastic sites and often found in very isolated locations. Yet they were in touch with world affairs through a network of highly active missionaries and travellers, of which two of the more familiar to us today are St Columba and St Killian. But disorder was soon to be the norm, generated by Viking raiding, internal strife and petty wars. The Vikings did gradually accept Christianity, although we have no building in the north that can be said to be of Viking origin.

Slowly, relative peace returned, but internal warfare remained a common feature of life, as one provincial king vied with another, sometimes making foreign alliances to win the day. Meanwhile, ecclesiastical sites continued to suffer and their treasures were carried off to pay for further wars.

Despite this unrest, continental influence increased and there were concerted efforts to re-establish order and conformity within the Irish church. The first continental architectural style to find its way to Ireland was the Romanesque. We do not have any very elaborate examples in the north, but there are substantial fragments at Maghera and Banagher in County Londonderry, at Kilmore in County Cavan, and on White Island in County Fermanagh. These sites, and many others in the south, became very influential in the late nineteenth century in the search for a 'national' style. Mainstream influences on the Irish church builders of the period were also generated from North Africa, Armenia and Turkey, as well as from Rome.

Gradually the Irish church began to conform to continental Roman-led practice. The Jewish calendar and eastern Christian observances were dropped, one by one, in favour of current Roman usage and, in the wake of these reforms, the continental monastic orders began to arrive on our shores. First to come were the Augustinians, Benedictines and Cistercians. Newry was the first continental foundation in the north, but nothing of its buildings are known to have survived.

Monasteries and friaries, like cathedrals, have very special characteristics which fall outside the parameters of this study; suffice to say that in Ulster we have some very substantial remains of several of these great houses, and it was more through these buildings, than in any other single route, that mainstream western architectural styles began to reach these shores.

The Main Forms and their Origins

The two root models for church buildings are the Temple in Jerusalem, which had most influence on the eastern churches, and the Roman Hall of Justice, or Basilica, in the form that it was adopted by the Emperor Constantine, when he legitimised and befriended Christianity in the year AD 313. Constantine himself, though he did not openly profess Christianity until on his deathbed, nevertheless personally directed the building of nine new churches in the basilica form in the city of Rome alone. It has to be said that, while in Ireland these formal influences were seriously felt, there continued a strong undercurrent that focused on building the simplest of vernacular shelters for everyday worship, all this paralleling the more articulated building forms of the continental-styled monastic houses.

The temple influence led to internal compartmentation of churches, reflecting the graduation of the temple courts and the veiled separation of the Holy of Holies. By contrast, the basilica is a large open space, formed of a nave and arcades and, beyond these, flanking aisles. At the one end is the main entrance and at the opposite end there is an apse, the floor of which is raised above the floor of the nave. In the centre of the apse is the seat of justice for the magistrate and, on each side, seating for his councillors, legal committee or presbytery. In front is the altar, and beyond, in the nave, is a low enclosure for the defending and opposing counsels. In use as a church, each of these features takes on a different, though related, significance. The altar went through another and separate development. In the early days of the church, Mass was often said at the tombs of the saints. It was an established pre-Christian Roman practice to share a meal with the dead. By degrees, it became the custom to enclose these tombs within a building and that building would naturally adopt the dedication of the saint in question. This practice led to the adoption of the pre-Christian Patrician form of two-storey tomb altar. Excavations below St Peter's in Rome have discovered rows of such tombs, including that of St Peter itself.

From this developed the two-storey church. The upper chamber is the church for everyday use where there is a stone table altar, in front of which a confessional connects to the undercroft church, and immediately below the high altar is the actual tomb of the saint or patron. Later churches not based around a tomb were endowed with relics that were deposited in the high altar.

Before the continental architectural forms had fully taken hold in Ireland another stylistic development had taken place – the 'Gothic' (or 'Gothick' in eighteenth century usage) had swept northern Europe . The exact origin of this style is unclear, but there are strong eastern influences that found their way westward, as a result of the crusades. Towers had also arrived from the east. In the Gothic monastic church building the chancel was adapted for the exclusive use of the members of the resident order. Orders made up of fully ordained priests led to the setting up of side altars, to facilitate the increasing number of Masses to be said. In the British Isles the apsidal east end gave way to a flat gable wall, against which the high altar came to be placed. From the provision of side altars there developed the cruciform plan.

An odd feature of many local ecclesiastical sites is that a series of buildings appear to have been erected, each one superseding the one before. An example is the Derry churches site just north of Portaferry, and another is Loughinisland, also in County Down. This sort of redevelopment has continued into modern times, so that surviving older churches are much more rare than one might expect. This is one of the main reasons that most of the surviving medieval buildings are ruins. Some of these ruins are very substantial, some others are fragments incorporated into later buildings. Downpatrick Cathedral represents the most substantial of these fragments. The loss was of course compounded by the effects of the Reformation and of warfare. A considerable number of medieval churches that had survived the Reformation were replaced by new buildings at a later date; that is to say, as soon as the congregation could afford to do so. The consequence of this is that any study of church buildings in use here has, in the main, to be about quite recent structures.

The Reformation, the Plantation and the Penal Laws

The first purpose-built church for the Reformed religion was St Patrick's in Newry, probably a little before the date of 1578 that is inscribed on a plaque inside the tower. The church building, as seen today, is largely the result of a full scale refurbishment in the 1820s. Luther's first purpose-built church, at Torgar, was erected in 1544. There were not many other new church buildings until the Plantations got underway. These were stone-built in a late Tudor Gothic style, although the occasional rash of classical detailing appears, as at Castlecaulfield. Most were plain halls, a few were aisled, but none were vaulted. The largest surviving building of this period is St Columb's Cathedral, Londonderry. It is recorded in many parishes that Anglicans and Roman Catholics continued to use the same buildings, albeit at different times, and the shared use of graveyards has continued to this day in many parishes. Hard times were soon to be visited on the newly-fledged Anglicans, firstly as a result of the 1641 rising and then at the hands of the Commonwealth. Recovery was slow, following the Williamite wars, because one important feature of the Reformation reorganisation had been the systematic syphoning off of church property into private hands. In short, even the Established Church had no firm or reliable form of income, leaving it very much dependent on patronage. However, the introduction of the Penal Laws, at the end of the seventeenth and beginning of the eighteenth century, ensured that for the next few decades the only new churches to be built would be for the Church of Ireland. Even so, there were not many new buildings erected, hence a considerable number of congregations continued to meet for divine service in market houses and other public buildings, as did their dissenting contemporaries.

Notwithstanding this scarcity of purpose-built church buildings, this was an era of lively philosophical thought, discussion and experimentation. As a result, there was no uniformity in the layout and furnishings of churches. The location of the holy table is constant against the east wall, protected by the rails campaigned for by William Laud, the future Archbishop of Canterbury, as early as 1616, when he was Dean of Gloucester. In Ulster it was the learned and devout Bishop Jeremy Taylor who oversaw this development. (Taylor was also responsible for the removal of dissenters from Anglican livings – not at all an easy task.) The Church of Ireland generally retained one Calvinist feature from its Commonwealth past, this being the celebration of the Eucharist from the Gospel end of the altar, rather than from the centre – the purpose of this practice was to have all movements visible to the congregation, in order that there could be no mystery or witchcraft at the holy table, and that nothing would be hidden from the people for whom the old Mass was now something to be condemned (see Article 28 of the 39 Articles of the Anglican Church). The increasing emphasis on preaching saw the pulpit frequently sited halfway down the nave, or in the centre of the nave aisle, thus bringing the Gospel as close as possible to the people. There was no chancel and no choir. If there was music it was provided for from a gallery over the west door, or to one side of the first structural bay at the east end. The font was occasionally to one side of the holy table at the east end, but more commonly close to the west door. The most usual seating pattern was to have pews or benches facing east on either side of a central aisle, but there are examples of the collegiate form, with the seats running parallel with the aisle instead of at right angles. The patron or landlord and his family would be provided with a private box pew, often with seating on all sides facing inwards, and very likely it would have its own fireplace. There do not appear to have been any rules about the location of this pew, some even having their own private doorways to the outside, to provide for a quick escape or a late entry! Seating was paid for, so that the poorest people might often be left standing in the aisles. The Church of Ireland was quite adventurous in construction methods and made early use of cast iron as a structural material.

Ascendancy and Enlightenment

To put its building programme onto a more firm footing, the Established Church in 1711 set up the

Board of First Fruits, whose task it was to accumulate a building fund from which the cost of new construction could be assisted. This Board continued in operation until 1833, when its responsibilities passed to the Irish Ecclesiastical Commissioners, and today these responsibilities rest with the Representative Church Body. Despite all such efforts, a substantial number of churches fell into seriously bad repair during the course of the eighteenth century, the problem not being solved until 1801 when, for the first time, Parliament began to provide central funds for church use.

Stylistically the Church of Ireland, in this period, at first adopted the style of the Classical Revival. It blended well with the Georgian terraces of the expanding towns and the palatial houses of the country gentry, but gradually this preference gave way to a Gothic as style that had classical proportions and Gothic ornamentation. The highly developed classical churches were largely an urban phenomenon, but when fashions changed most of these were taken down and replaced, as the new Gothic Revival swept the country. A number of architects were employed in drafting plans in this Gothic style: for example, Michael Shanahan for the Earl Bishop of Derry and Thomas Cooley for Archbishop Robinson of Armagh.

The Presbyterians were the largest dissenting denomination in Ulster and had received official favours under the government of the Commonwealth. However, this was not to last and the introduction of the Penal Laws was a severe handicap. The government of Charles II applied a carrot as well as a stick to the problem, and in 1672 granted to the Presbyterians in Ireland the *Regium Donum*. This was the first ever regular payment in modern times to any church from public funds. The payment was withdrawn in 1710, but reintroduced by George I at an increased rate. This favourable arrangement lasted unbroken until 1869. It was also the case that the Penal Laws were not stringently implemented and as the century wore on the practice became ever more liberal. The standing of the Presbyterian community improved again in 1780 with the repeal of the Test Act, removing the bar to holding civil and military office under the Crown. A rash of substantial meeting houses sprung up as a result. These structures, and the handful that predate them, vary greatly in size but, large or small, they share a distinct vernacular character. Formal architecture was deliberately avoided and was only manifest in the occasional detail, as in the casing of an entrance door. Internal arrangements were fairly consistent. The seating focused on the pulpit, which was so placed as to be in the closest possible communion with the congregation. The most common placing in a rectangular building was in the centre of the long wall. To accommodate more people, galleries were added and, in many cases, an outshot wing was extended facing the pulpit to create a 'T' plan. The first such 'T' plan meeting house is recorded in 1636, at Anstruther in Scotland.

In Ulster, two particularly remarkable meeting houses survive from this period, one in Rosemary Street, Belfast, and the other in Randalstown (page 39). These have an elliptical plan and have generated a great deal of historical speculation and debate, but it seems likely that the form is of Huguenot origin and the installation of galleries may have the same beginnings. There are no similar Huguenot churches that survive, but it is well documented that there were three such in Lyons alone until they were destroyed, following the revocation of the Edict of Nantes in 1685. At this time the Sacraments were received at tables specially set up in the aisles. For this purpose a wide transverse aisle or space was left in front of the pulpit. Aisles amongst the seating were almost never central, an arrangement that deliberately denied a ritualistic approach to liturgy. In later times this form for taking the Sacraments was superseded and they were more often brought to the people seated in their own pews from a small table set up below the pulpit, where they were first blessed by the minister. This area in front of the pulpit became progressively more problematic with the adoption of choirs. The Presbyterian congregation in Ireland went into schism in 1726 over the Westminister Confession of Faith. It has been mainly the non-subscribing congregations that have retained their meeting houses in their original form.

Most other dissenting denominations followed Presbyterian building practice through this period, but this was not the case with the Society of Friends (the Quakers). It would appear that denominational adherence followed quite distinct social and class delineations. Francis McCorry in his study *Lurgan: An Irish Provincial Town 1610–1970* takes up this point, as do a number of other historians. The membership of the Friends seems to have been drawn almost exclusively from commerce and manufacturing. Their meeting houses each served a relatively large geographical area and a tradition grew up for one congregation to extend an invitation to another, so that on occasions there were quite large social gatherings to cater for at a single meeting site. In consequence, as well as the meeting house, there were lodgings, stables etc. The first meeting house in the north of Ireland was opened in Lurgan in 1654. Like the Presbyterians, formal architectural styles were avoided and the vernacular was favoured, but there the similarity ends. The internal arrangements have no focus, because there is no minister nor any formal arrangement for receiving the Sacraments.

In the Grange Meeting House (see page 121), as in most of the older meeting houses, there is an elders' gallery. This stretches the full width of the primary hall. The most striking feature is the planned flexibility of use. Again, following the example of Grange, there is what could be termed the primary meeting room, occupying roughly half the volume of the building. The other half of the building can be shuttered off for separate independent meetings and comprises two spaces, a mezzanine or gallery and a space below it. The stairs to the gallery are partitioned off in such a way that their use will not disturb the activities in any of the three meeting spaces. This is all very ingenious and very simple. The landscape and setting were as carefully considered as the buildings, thus creating a harmonious environment. To be a Friend was a way of life – life itself was the true and only Sacrament and so it is not surprising to find the clear expression of this belief in the planning for a total community, as at the mill village of Bessbrook in County Armagh.

Here the Richardson family laid out the whole settlement in accordance with philanthropic Quaker principles, long before it became generally accepted to think along these lines at all.

The same community approach can be seen in the planning of Gracehill by the Moravians, about a hundred years earlier. At the Gracehill site the spirit of community was no doubt born of the harsh experience of a colonial lifestyle in the New World – although the movement originated in Bohemia, their ideas reached Ireland via America. Gracehill is an exceptionally harmonious composition of regularly proportioned buildings and sympathetically regulated open space. It is remarkable now – when it was built it must have been quite extraordinary and a stark contrast to the living conditions and standards of the majority of the local population. This Moravian church building is in Queen Anne style, with just enough formal detail to make it distinct from its secular neighbours. There is a strong classical symmetry, both inside and out. Again the focus is on the long wall and the building is galleried, so bringing a maximum number of people into direct proximity to the Sacraments, the Word and the minister. A characteristic of Moravian planning is to have the minister's lodging integral to the church building itself. This is not, however, unique to this denomination.

In the eighteenth century, Roman Catholic purpose-built Mass houses were necessarily few and far between, but there are examples still standing, as at Portaferry, where the chapel was originally constructed in 1704. It has to be acknowledged that the building, as it stands today, is much changed; nevertheless, the original building is in fact still there, buried among a proliferation of extensions and alterations, as can be verified by comparing the building outlined on maps over the years. Like the other nonconformists, Roman Catholic congregations, at first, chose the vernacular, rather than any formal architectural style. The plan form of many pre-emancipation chapels is closely modelled on Presbyterian practice of the time, bringing the focus to the centre of the long wall. Here the altar is placed, where in Protestant churches there would have been a pulpit. Even 'T'-plan chapels were once quite common, but most of these early buildings have long since been replaced by architectural set pieces of a later tradition. A few survive and are historically very precious; a fine example is the one illustrated from Lisbane (page 86), in the Ards, used now for Mass only once a year, on the night of All Souls, the regular daily function having passed, since 1876, to the chapel of St Joseph at Ballycran. The extreme simplicity and directness of this neat little building must once have been commonplace. One west door serves all. The priest robes in a compartment at the back of the confessional, itself a rare survivor of a type once common, where only the priest is totally enclosed. The penitent kneels against the outside, communicating through a small aperture. At the time this Mass house was built the church was served by a relatively few dedicated clergy who had been educated abroad. The Penal Laws were patchily implemented and, as the century wore on, were honoured more in the breach than in the observation. In 1795 the Dublin government supported the founding of St Patrick's College, Maynooth, as a Catholic seminary. So was heralded a new era and a new attitude to and within the Church. Emancipation followed in 1829. Right across the country, sites for new churches were sold or donated by landlords and subscribed to by numerous Protestant patrons. The new buildings were very different from the old, being distinctly architectural. In the south, Classical Revival styles were popular, but in the north late Gothic styles were more often chosen.

Out of the midst of this period of change, worldwide political unrest and even revolution, the Wesleyan Methodist movement emerged. The beginnings were contained within the Established Church. Wesley, himself an ordained minister of the Anglican Church, died so. In 1818 his followers divided. The primitive movement continued his customs and received the Sacraments at their parish churches. The meeting houses they built are quite distinctive, simple gabled halls, stone-built, sometimes rendered and usually with semicircular-headed windows. In 1878 the movement was reunited and this coincided with an enormous expansion in congregations. New churches were built everywhere, right across the province. In format, most of these late nineteenth century buildings are very similar to the galleried Presbyterian meeting houses of the time. The body of the church is more or less square and has a vestibule the full width of the front wall, housing stairways to the galleries. Against the back wall is the organ and in front of it the pulpit, communion table and choir box. The choir box is of course omitted in the smaller churches, where there was no choir. Ulster Methodist congregations were not infected by the stylistic epidemic of the Gothic Revival and generally retained classical forms and afterwards adopted the Free Styles of the twentieth century.

The War of Styles

Going back to the beginning of the nineteenth century, all the main groupings were now abandoning the vernacular and began to settle for formal architectural styles. The choices they made say a great deal about the outlook and aspirations of their congregations. The Church of Ireland continued with its simple Gothic style and, for the first time receiving substantial financial help from the government, began an extensive building programme. The aim was to provide a church building within reasonable distance of everyone. The Presbyterians adopted the classical Greek Revival style and there is little doubt that this was a decision inspired by the great significance attached to the provision of a quality education, naturally based on the classics. Many Presbyterian academies were set up, the most famous of which is the Royal Belfast Academical Institution. Meanwhile, the Roman Catholic Church in Ulster favoured the late Gothic style, that is the Perpendicular and Tudor Revival styles. The choice of these styles may have been influenced by the Plantation churches of the Church of Ireland, because in the south classical forms were more commonly employed and of course the fashionable Georgian suburbs of Dublin and other major cities and towns had been graced with matching Protestant classical designs. By the mid-nineteenth century the vernacular, as a choice for church buildings, had gone forever and, waiting in the wings, a new architectural fashion was about to sweep all before it – the Gothic Revival.

An interest in everything medieval seemed to affect the whole of cultural life throughout the British Isles; landed families searched every dusty corner to find a shining medieval armoured knight somewhere in their past and coats of arms sprung up everywhere, like the harvest from the Gorgon's teeth. The new architectural style was applied regardless of function, but it has to be said that some extremely beautiful buildings did emerge, and of course it is hardly surprising that most of these were churches. After all, this was the purpose for which the original Gothic had been developed.

In church work the new interest in Gothic architecture can be traced to the founding of the Tractarian movement in 1833. In 1841 this group began to publish a periodical, *The Ecclesiologist*. Out of this rarefied atmosphere there emerged, from the smoking incense, Welby Northmore Pugin. In 1834 he converted to Roman Catholicism and began a relentless crusade to establish Gothic as the only fit style for any new Christian church. His first major project in Ireland was to extend the seminarian college in Maynooth, where the work began in 1845. The Roman Catholic hierarchy were quickly won over to such an extent that Henry Newman found it all but impossible to build in the Byzantine style when he proposed a chapel for the Catholic University in Dublin. Welby's son, Edwin, set up his architectural practice in Cork. The fire spread rapidly northwards, championed in the works of JJ McCarthy. His St Patrick's, Dungannon (page 123), and St Joseph's, Carrickmacross (page 114), are illustrated, but his most important contribution is without doubt the Catholic Cathedral in Armagh.

This period is also marked by the emergence of the practice, by congregations, of employing architects of their own faith. This had not been the case for the previous generation. Thomas Duff and Thomas Jackson, for example, had worked freely across the sectarian divides, but now new battle lines were drawn and the architecture of the time reflected this. Many Church of Ireland congregations favoured the architectural firm of Lanyon, Lynn and Lanyon, while the Ecclesiastical Commissioners employed Welland and Gillespie. The Presbyterians sought the services of Young and MacKenzie. However, the first Presbyterian church (Unitarian) in the new style was by the architect William Barre, dated 1852, and sited in his home town of Newry. Newry is an important place for ecclesiastical firsts – the site of the first continental style monastic house in the north; the first purpose-built church for the Reformed faith (St Patrick's); and the first of all the new generation of Roman Catholic cathedrals in Ulster (St Patrick's and St Colman's). The Gothic Revival style was, however, totally unsuited to Presbyterian worship – its adoption as a style was pure fashion. It created quite the wrong sort of space, so that the architects were led into all sorts of contortions to make their designs work.

In the Church of Ireland the new style went hand in hand with a liturgical re-ordering, so that in this instance the new buildings did work, although there are plenty of records of congregations opposing the changes. Indeed, there was street rioting in Belfast to oppose what many referred to as 'Ritualism'. Existing Anglican churches were given new chancels, often adorned with highly symbolic decoration. Pulpits were resited on the Gospel side at the chancel steps and holy tables were exchanged for stone altars, often raised on a dais and approached by three symbolic steps. Not all churches were altered, so that we can still experience the earlier forms. Here illustrated is the parish church at Boho (page 93) and the more architectural St John's, Clondehorky (page 75). Of the cathedrals, only Clogher has retained the earlier Calvinistic form.

Other changes were also taking place. In 1869 the Church of Ireland was faced with disestablishment and the loss of most of its income. At the same parliamentary stroke, the Presbyterian Church was deprived of the *Regium Donum*. Both these churches made serious attempts to relate to an Irish identity. The bible and prayer books had been translated into Irish and in a few places services were conducted in Irish. The Church of Ireland began to develop a national architectural style, using a version of Hiberno Romanesque and making clear architectural references to the early Irish Church. Included in the illustrated examples are St Patrick's, Jordanstown (page 40) and (although later) St Patrick's, Saul (page 91).

Following the famine, the Roman Catholic Church set aside the memory of the anti-clerical atrocities of the French Revolution to become gradually identified with the new Irish nationalist and republican movements. One reason may have been that the now mature first generation of priests, educated at Maynooth, had not been exposed to the strong anti-clerical politics of mainland Europe that their predecessors had been. In the same way that the Anglican Church had developed its identity as an Irish Church, the Roman Catholic Church also began to turn to a version of Hiberno Romanesque. A freak coincidence highlights just this point. It relates to the fine Hiberno Romanesque church designed by Ashlin and Colman for Cloghoge, south of Newry, dedicated to the Sacred Heart, where the first Mass was said on Easter Sunday 1916, the day before the Easter Rising.

Experimentation and Uncertainty

A feature that marks out late nineteenth century and early twentieth century church building is the development of an unprecedented level of artistry. This too is a potential study in its own right, but every age has left us craftsmanship of very high quality – the work of the medieval masons; the beautiful plaster work, joinery and funeral monuments of the seventeenth and eighteenth centuries; and in this later phase there develops an intensity of excellence in furnishings and artistic works, only matched by the High Gothic of medieval times. The buildings chosen illustrate these points are St Mark's, Holywood Road, Belfast (pages 23–4, 61); St Patrick's, Jordanstown (page 40); the Chapel of The Convent of Mercy, Enniskillen (pages 94–5); All Souls, Elmwood Avenue, Belfast (page 53); and my own special favourite – the Chapel of St Mary, The Immaculate Mother of God, at St Colman's

College, Newry (pages 50–1). In the latter building there is a feast of artistic delight – particularly the coloured glass and decorative tile work of Richard King from the workshop of Harry Clarke; and the subtle Art Deco rendering of perfectly traditional Romanesque building forms by the architect John Robinson.

As the twentieth century progressed different architects took centre stage. In the case of the Church of Ireland, the massive undertaking for the building of a new cathedral in Belfast was a major focus right throughout the century. The designing began in the 1890s and is not quite finished yet. A more modest work by the same architect, Thomas Drew, is St Donard's, Dundrum (see page 84). The giants in the Roman Catholic scene have been Padriac Gregory and Liam McCormick, both represented in the case notes. For the Presbyterians, John MacGeagh did great work; regretfully, none is included here. However, works by Ferguson and McIlveen and Gordon McKnight are included.

Today, church building continues apace in the face of increasing uncertainty regarding liturgies, dogmas and doctrines. As always, architecture holds the mirror up to life, and in many new church buildings we now see reflected the clutter and disorder of our everyday existence. No longer do the churches speak of that eternal changeless order that brings rest to our souls and troubled minds. New shapes and forms are continually put to the test, with varying degrees of success or failure. A few are very beautiful, quite as beautiful as anything from our a past. The ability to build for the love and glory of God has not quite left us yet.

Conclusion

Different people see churches in different ways and expect different things of them. Among all these differences there is one constant – it is that a church is a special place.

It seems to me that it makes no great difference whether the building is magnificent or humble – it has only met its brief if it is made perfect in what it set out to be. In the same way that the words of a prayer are carefully chosen and the music gives emphasis to enhance the meaning of those words, so the building creates the environment for worship. All these elements must be harmonious with the one intent. Thus the building must, without any word of explanation, make the visitor, whether or not he or she is a Christian, fully aware that here is a very special place.

Into the Future: Threats and Alternatives

Churches have been put to all manner of uses through history – as stables, arsenals, quarters for troops, libraries, concert halls and so on. The issue is not a new one. The difference between the present and the past is that today changes in the use of buildings are regulated and require planning approval. A great many church buildings are further protected by listing as "buildings of special architectural or historic interest". As I have remarked already, in most of our communities the church buildings are among the most significant architectural statements, so that their loss or major alteration will also change the character of the wider environment.

In the past, churches that no longer had a use were either demolished or remained as ruins. There are many ruined churches in our countryside from every age. To keep these ruins is comparable to the laying up of military colours. They become symbolic of the passing of time and the transitory nature of our own existence. A few church buildings have been deliberately kept as ruins even in our time (for example, the old cathedral in Coventry), but these are exceptional cases. Strangely, although the consumer society is generally a society that encourages disposable and transitory solutions, the contemporary attitude is different when it comes to church buildings. One reason for this may be that the approach to new building design is generally utilitarian and basic; so that where a church is threatened with extinction it is unlikely that anything of the same architectural quality will ever be put in its place, whatever the planning policy for the area may be.

So if redundant churches are to be kept what are the most suitable uses for which they can by adapt-ed? Generally speaking, the uses that are closest in character to the original will be most successful. In some areas there is a reluctance to allow church buildings to pass into the hands of another denomination or religion, but from every practical point of view this will be the best way to conserve the building. If this option is not available then the next best will be a use that shares the same basic principle, ie a community function requiring a single individual space. Examples would be a theatre, concert hall, library, art gallery, museum or council chamber. Obviously there are quite small churches that will provide quite modest accommodation, such as the Methodist church at Wheathill (page 98) and the Church of Ireland at Forkhill (page 47), which are now in use as dwellings. However, most churches are not domestic in scale. If the only uses that can be found do require compartmentation, then the most successful approach will be to aim for a totally separate structure to provide the division of the space and simply treat the parent church building as a shelter. This will allow the secondary structure to be removed or further altered without affecting the structural integrity of the parent building. If this approach is not followed, as through time other alternative user requirements come forward and lead to further changes and modifications, the original building will be progressively compromised until it eventually becomes, in every practical sense, useless. These are some possible ways in which the conservation of the exteriors of redundant church buildings can be achieved. Interiors are much more difficult, and the difficulties vary so much from site to site that no sensible guidelines that have a general application are really possible.

There is little doubt that reuse is a problem that will not go away. Congregations who are anticipating moving should start planning for the reuse of their church long before they close the door after the last service. Nothing makes a building less attractive and unlikely to find a new use than a period of neglect. Reuse is never a cheap option, and to needlessly add the burden of massive repairs and reinstatement will often rule it out of the economic capability of any prospective new user. The Society of Friends in Lurgan planned in advance, before their move to new premises, and their forethought has certainly reaped dividends. If situations like this are discussed in advance, it can often transpire that a new use will be found within the congregation itself.

Like the Devil in his pursuit of man, threats to the future of church buildings frequently come in disguise. There is a growing tendency to build halls and other community buildings in close relationship to church buildings. While it may seem difficult to raise the initial capital, it is often nearly impossible to go on raising the money for ongoing management and maintenance. One cannot help but conclude that some congregations are burdening themselves with liabilities which, in the long term, they will not be able to honour; and that these liabilities, finally, may well pose the greatest threat of all to the continuing existence of the church itself. If a hall is detached but convenient, it can be sold off as a separate entity if and when the need arises. Perhaps the church building itself can be adapted to provide for worship and community use. All these issues require serious thought.

Another threat to churches, but of a different kind, is the motor car. The settings of so many of our beautiful church buildings have been totally destroyed in a sea of tarmac. In urban locations churches of different denominations are often sited quite close together and in other situations schools and churches are closely related. In these locations more thought could be given to sharing facilities. Perhaps local councils would be in the best position to encourage this style of cooperation. Certainly, churches seem to be increasingly inclined to let out their parking spaces to other car users during the week. This at least cuts down on the need for tarmaced parks elsewhere.

Other congregations appeal that they lack resources, while they often own other property that could provide badly needed income, if only it were to be more imaginatively managed.

There is much food for thought here. Indeed, not only thought but action. The overriding goal must be to make sure that, whatever else happens, the church building itself continues to symbolise and to provide for meaningful and dignified worship.

The welcoming entrance to the Old Congregation Presbyterian Church in Randalstown, Co Antrim (see page 39).

The Old Congregation Presbyterian Church in Randalstown, Co Antrim (see page 39).

The Archbishop's private chapel in Armagh (see page 43).

St Patrick's Church of Ireland Cathedral, Armagh. The recumbent monuments are to Archbishops Marcus Gervais Beresford and Lord John Beresford (see page 45).

St Malachy's Roman Catholic Church in Camlough, Co Armagh (see page 45).

A view of the altar and surroundings in St Brigid's Roman Catholic Church, Glassdrummon, Crossmaglen, Co Armagh (see page 47).

The Abbey at St John's Church of Ireland, Kilcluney, Co Armagh (see page 48).

Two interior views of St Colman's College Chapel in Newry. Note the gallery projections, the opus sectile stations and the side altar to St Teresa of Lisieux (see page 50).

All Souls Non-Subscribing Presbyterian Church, Elmwood Avenue, Belfast (see page 53).

The First Church of Christ the Scientist, Rugby Road, Belfast (see page 56).

St Mark's Church of Ireland on the Holywood Road in Belfast (see page 61).

Interior view of St Mark's Church of Ireland (left) and St Mary's Dominican Convent (right) (see pages 61–2).

Tennent Street
Baptist Church,
Belfast
(see page 63).

Expressions of faith in Co Cavan
– the Church of Ireland parish
church in Cavan town (above, see
page 68) and St Mary's Roman
Catholic Church in Belturbet
(right, see page 67).

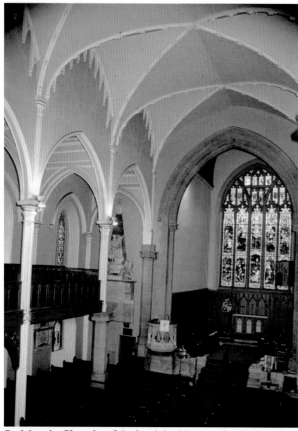

St Mary's Church of Ireland in Newry, Co Down (see page 88).

A detail of the interior of Boho Church of Ireland, Co Fermanagh (see page 93).

The tiled floor of the Priory at Killadeas in Co Fermanagh (see page 100).

St Swithin's Church of Ireland in Magherafelt, Co Londonderry (see page 107).

TO THE GLORY OF GOD & IN MEMORY OF
FRANCES ARMSTRONG
BORN MARCH 6TH 1803 DIED JVNE 4TH 1883

A dedicatory window in Christ Church, Castlerock, Co Londonderry (see page 104).

St Peter's Church of Ireland, Templeport, Co Cavan (see page 73).

The Methodist Church in Donegal town (see page 76).

St Mura's Church of Ireland in Fahan (see page 79).

The simple interior of Lettermacaward Church of Ireland, Co Donegal (see page 79).

Lisdonan Roman Catholic Church, Carrickmacross, Co Monaghan (see page 113).

St Joseph's, Carrickmacross, Co Monaghan, displays the impressive stained glass of Richard King from the studio of Harry Clarke (see page 114).

St Muadhan's Church of Ireland, Errigal Truagh, Co Monaghan (see page 117).

St Patrick's Roman Catholic Church in Dungannon, Co Tyrone (see page 122).

First Presbyterian Church, Strabane, Co Tyrone (see page 126).

The cathedral-like proportions of the Sacred Heart Roman Catholic Church in Omagh, Co Tyrone (see page 126).

County Antrim

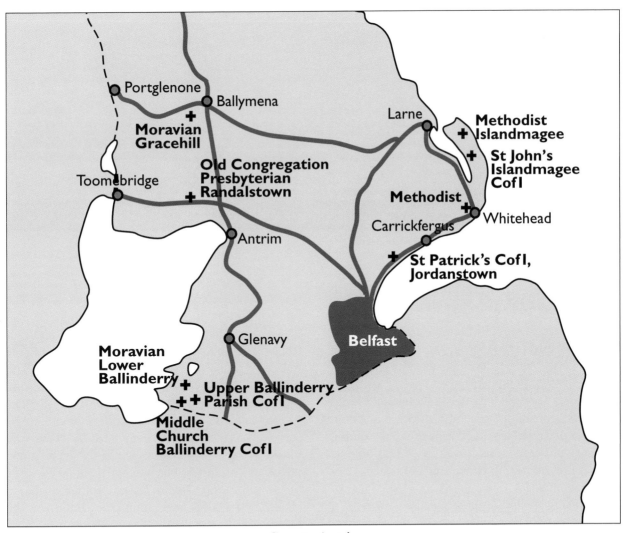

County Antrim

The Middle Church, Church of Ireland, Ballinderry.

BALLINDERRY

The Middle Church, Church of Ireland

The Middle Church was built in 1666 by the restoration Bishop of Down and Connor, Jeremy Taylor, whose funeral hatchment now hangs in the church. The building was extensively restored in 1902 by a team led by the antiquarian Francis Joseph Bigger. While some of his work is not quite true to today's conservation standards, the building remains substantially as it was when built and, as such, it is extremely important both historically and architecturally.

The plan is a single uninterrupted cell, entered at the west end below a gallery that is itself accessed by an external flight of stone stairs, set against the north wall. There is no ceiling, while the floor is paved in stone and the fittings are all stained oak.

The holy table is against the east wall, raised by one step and protected by a simple timber railing. The three-decker pulpit for rector, curate and clerk had just become an accepted feature of Church of Ireland churches at this time, but this one is a very rare survivor. Most were removed during the late nineteenth century liturgical reforms. The position on the long north wall, in the centre of the congregation, emphasises the contemporary importance of preaching. This was the plan location chosen by most nonconformist congregations for the next one and a half centuries, but without the dual focus of the eastern holy table. Many Roman Catholic chapels were also set to this plan, but since the Sacrament is the focus of the Mass, the altar replaced the pulpit on the long wall. The positioning of church furnishings was intensely disputed all across the United Kingdom at this time, and the differing opinions led to some unusual solutions. The arrangement seen at Ballinderry, however, became widely accepted and was in line with the Laudian principles upheld by Jeremy Taylor in the face of Calvinistic pressures and more extreme Protestant opinions.

The beautiful lychgate is entirely the work of the restorers.

(See also front cover.)

Moravian

The first Moravian building on the site dated from 1755. The present church was built in 1836 to replace the earlier construction, which had been burnt the previous year.

This is a more modest building than Gracehill (see below) and obviously in the vernacular tradition.

Interior view of the Middle Church, Church of Ireland, Ballinderry.

The Moravian Church in Lower Ballinderry.

The Church of Ireland parish church in Upper Ballinderry.

Like Gracehill and Kilwarlin, the manse is integrated with the church and the two share a common plan. The result, including gardens and graveyard, is a very significant feature in the landscape and local community, making a greater impact than its size might suggest.

Parish Church, Church of Ireland

This is a text book Church of Ireland church of the period (built in 1824), both inside and out. At a time when towers and chancels were being added to the earlier single-cell hall churches, this building has them all as original pieces. It also has windows on both the north and south walls, whereas the earlier hall churches normally had windows on one side only. This allowed for the pulpit to be centred on the long wall, where there were no windows. The new form, with chancel and pulpit adjacent to the chan-cel arch, reflected an increase in the frequency of parish communion and a greater emphasis on the Sacraments. An interesting structural feature is the use of cast iron in the construction of the gallery. (The Church of Ireland was quite adventurous in the use of this new material and it became a feature of many new and altered churches at this time.) The building is carefully sited on a rise in the ground and enclosed by an elegant plantation of trees.

An inscribed stone in the tower of this church explains that the costs of construction were jointly met by the Marquis of Hertford and the parish.

GRACEHILL
Moravian

This church was built in 1765, with the construction overseen by John Reinhard Schloezer. It was ceilinged in 1767 and the organ was installed in

The Moravian Church in Gracehill, centred on one side of a formally laid-out square.

1781. Other improvements took place in 1798 and the whole building was refurnished and refloored in 1842.

The origins of the Moravians are to be found in Prague and the teachings of John Hus. Subsequent religious persecution led to the mass emigration of his followers, with the first Moravians reaching Ireland via the United States. This followed the visit to Dublin of John Cennick in 1746. The management structure of the church is episcopal. There are five congregations in Northern Ireland, all of which have church buildings of note (see also Ballinderry, page 35). These are very much the focus of their respective communities.

This particular church is a rectangular building, with the pulpit and holy table central to the long wall, facing the two entrances. Although the pulpit appears to dominate the table, the service is conducted from the table and the pulpit is only used for preaching. The pulpit in this case is an extremely elegant piece of furniture. The building does have architectural features, such as the classical door cases, but in conception it is a vernacular meeting house, peaceful and serene in a totally ordered landscape of buildings and trees. The manse is attached to the church, with a direct connecting door. Behind the building there is stabling – a reminder that some members of the congregation, living outside the settlement, would have travelled considerable distances to attend.

ISLANDMAGEE
St John's, Church of Ireland

This church was built in 1609 or earlier. In 1828 it was made smaller by the removal of the north aisle and about 28 feet from the west end. In 1988 a combined vestry and porch were added.

This modest, matter of fact building is typical of the early Plantation churches of the Church of Ireland, very few of which have survived and certainly very few of which are in such original condition. Although Jacobean, it displays quite definite late Tudor Gothic characteristics. The internal space is a simple hall with no spatial demarcations or compartmentation.

The plantation of trees associated with the graveyard is characteristic of the period and makes a strong feature in the landscape.

St John's, Church of Ireland, Islandmagee.

Wesleyan Methodist

Built in 1829, this is a vernacular building with no architectural pretensions, but well proportioned on an eye-catching bend in the road.

The building is very nearly square, with a lobbied entrance in the centre of the south wall. The seating is in three blocks, providing for two aisles. The dais and its furnishings are not original, but the layout has not been changed. The adjoining cottages were almost certainly built as a manse.

Window alterations and the felling of the trees that previously graced the site have not helped the overall impression, but these features could easily be restored.

The Methodist Church in Islandmagee.

RANDALSTOWN
Presbyterian Old Congregation

Built in 1790, the architect of Randalstown Presbyterian Old Congregation church is unknown. The walls were very skillfully raised in 1929 to give more room in the galleries, at which time the elliptical attic windows and a minister's room were added. The loss of the original Gothic windows in the course of this work is to be regretted.

While the building is very striking, it is quite definitely conceived in the old plain meeting house tradition and is not in any formal architectural style. It is the overall elliptical form that catches the eye and this has caused a great deal of discussion. Charles Brett and Tommy Nicolls draw comparisons with St Andrew's Church in Edinburgh and the Rosemary Street Presbyterian church in Belfast.

Another influence may have been the Huguenots, who came to Ireland in large numbers in the seven-

Interior view of the Methodist Church in Islandmagee.

teenth century to escape persecution in France. In the sixteenth century, in Lyons, they were known to have built three elliptical churches, with plain functional exteriors – a style reflected in the building in

The Presbyterian Old Congregation Church in Randalstown, with the Church of Ireland in the background.

Randalstown. A list of the names of the congregation of the time could provide some clues.

The sweeping curves of the exterior are reflected in the interior fittings and furnishings, providing an unobstructed focus on the minister, and his message, in his raised desk, opposite the main door. It is without doubt one of the outstanding gems of church building in Ulster and makes an interesting comparison with the profile of the parish church, sited only a few hundred yards away (see photograph on facing page).

(See also colour section, page 17.)

JORDANSTOWN
St Patrick's, Church of Ireland

Built between 1866 and 1868, this church was designed by WH Lynn of Lanyon, Lynn and Lanyon.

The furnishing of the sanctuary was not completed until 1894 and the very fine sculpture of St Patrick as a slave boy, set into the tympanum of the porch, dates from 1933. At this period, leading up to disestablishment, the Church of Ireland made a distinct effort to be Irish and this design is one of the best illustrations of this movement. The inspiration for the design came from Teampull Finghin in Clonmacnoise, County Offaly, a twelfth century nave and chancel in Irish Romanesque style, with an earlier round tower incorporated on the south side. The features of the Jordanstown church that best reflect this influence are the round tower, here used as a vestry, the south entrance doorcase and the chancel arch. One also wonders if the almost contemporary St Finbarr's Cathedral in Cork had any influence on Lynn as he designed this church.

The impressive exterior of St Patrick's Church of Ireland, Jordanstown.

The Methodist Church in Whitehead.

Elsewhere in the building there is a very strong Byzantine flavour, in both form and detail. The layout is ecclesiological and contains a wealth of symbolism. The intensity of the design is remarkable, with practically nothing left to chance. The whole assembly is set off by a number of particular works of art of the very highest quality. This is without doubt one of the most completely beautiful church buildings in the whole of Ireland.

WHITEHEAD Methodist

This is an interesting 'T' plan building, designed by H Sykes, which is unusual for its date (built in 1900). It is a confident design in the Arts and Crafts style that makes continual references to the late perpendicular Gothic, especially in the design of the fenestration. There are novelties, in particular the arrangement of window openings in the south gable where there are three elongated rectangles with a central occulus above, all bound together by a common hood mould. Altogether this composition is an unusual one for this denomination. The church shares a boundary wall and gates with the manse, and taken together presents a well-ordered unity.

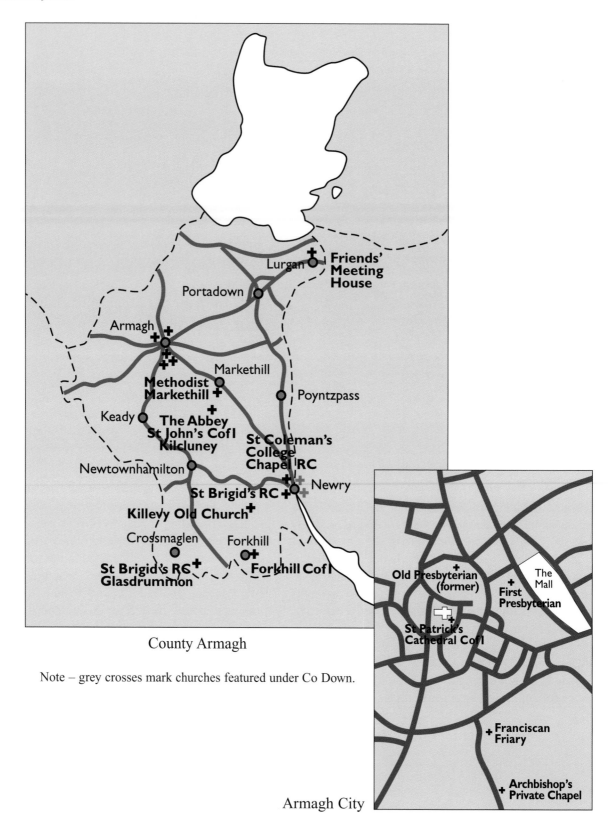

County Armagh

Note – grey crosses mark churches featured under Co Down.

Armagh City

County Armagh

ARMAGH CITY
The Archbishop's Private Chapel, Church of Ireland

Built between the years 1781 and 1786, this chapel was originally designed by Thomas Cooley and completed, after Cooley's death, by Francis Johnston.

The building fulfilled two roles: firstly and most importantly as a chapel; but secondly as a classical ornament to the landscaping of the new demesne, created by Archbishop Robinson soon after his translation to the primacy in 1765.

There are not many Anglican churches in the classical style in Ulster. This building is particularly beautiful in its scholarship and proportion and is of a quality that elevates it to a European importance. Yet the architectural space within has a great deal in common with the many parish churches built all over Ireland at the time (see Boho parish church, page 93). One feature that makes it quite different from these other churches is the collegiate plan, where the stalls face each other across a central space. The entrance way is quite confined, giving a greater appreciation of the space beyond. Over the entrance passage is a

The Archbishop's Chapel, set in the grounds of Armagh City and District Council.

musicians' gallery and in the far wall a shallow sanctuary. Except in the sanctuary, the furnishings are original. There is no evidence that there was ever a pulpit.

(See also colour section, page 18.)

First Presbyterian, The Mall

This congregation had previously met in the Abbey Street meeting house (see below, page 45) before the new building was constructed in 1878, with Young and MacKenzie employed as architects. The contrast in style and basic format between the two buildings could hardly be greater. Whereas the Abbey Street building has no architectural pretensions – even its Gothic windows were alterations made after the first Presbyterian congregation had moved out. Here on the Mall is a full-blown Gothic Revival building, set out on the long axis and with strongly episcopalian overtones.

There is one significant difference from the other Young and MacKenzie church illustrated, Fitzroy in Belfast (see page 57), in that from the outside the building form makes it quite clear that inside there is a galleried hall, not an aisled, cruciform plan, as might be expected from the architectural style chosen.

The Franciscan Friary

Founded in 1264, suppressed in 1542, and partly destroyed in 1595, this is one of the most significant ecclesiastical ruins in Northern Ireland. The foundation is the same as that of the cathedral, rebuilt at roughly the same time, and by record remained an 'Irish' house, so many in Ireland being manned principally by English and French recruits. Note in particular the nearly central location of the crossing of the cruciform plan. This is a common feature of friaries in Ireland, with the friars using the chancel almost as a private chapel, while in the nave a separate altar may have been sited for the use of the laity. The remains were later incorporated into the landscaping of the Church of Ireland Archbishop's demesne, where they featured as a fashionable romantic ruin.

The First Presbyterian Church, which faces on to the Mall in Armagh city.

The remains of the Franciscan Friary in Armagh city.

Presbyterian, Abbey Street (former)

The church in Abbey Street was built 1722. The architect is not known. It stands on the ancient site of the Abbey of St Peter and St Paul. Dean Swift, watching the construction in hand, reported that much of the stone used came from the Abbey ruins, although the builders took the trouble to chisel "the Popery out of the very stones".

The Old Presbyterian Church in Abbey Street, Armagh, now owned and operated by the local council.

The plan form is a 'T', comparable to Camlough Roman Catholic chapel (below) and Fountain Street Presbyterian church in Downpatrick (page 84), both illustrated here. Around 1900 the galleries were altered, together with the windows and external staircases. The Presbyterian congregation having built other premises, this building was put to a number of secular uses and presently forms part of Armagh City and District Council's St Patrick's Trian development.

St Patrick's Cathedral, Church of Ireland

The present form of the cathedral relates, in the main, to the rebuilding of 1268–70 on the part of Archbishop O'Scannail. The justification for including a cathedral in a book about churches is that this building has the longest continuous Christian history of any ecclesiastical building in Northern Ireland. Much has already been written about the cathedral, so there is no advantage in competing with any earlier author in these few short pages. Suffice to say that despite continual attacks, burnings and desecrations, not to mention renovations and re-orderings, this building has remained remarkably intact and, as such, is a signal emblem of Christianity in despair as well as triumph – a not irrelevant message to Christians of today.

Worth noting is the misalignment of the nave with the chancel. Several suggestions have been put forward for this – bearing in mind that builders who could construct a building of this scale and magnitude could certainly draw a straight line – of these explanations the one that is most reasonable is that this is a symbol deliberately incorporated to demonstrate the imperfection of man in the sight of the Almighty. In the logic of those who made the cathedral, it would be sinful to praise the work of the builders before recognising the perfection of God.

This building contains some of the most beautiful funeral monuments in all of our Ulster churches.

(See also colour section, page 19.)

CAMLOUGH
St Malachy's, Roman Catholic

Built in 1816, according to the date stone over the west door, the style and plan suggest that this building could be much older. Could it be that the date only relates to the entrance porch? The 'T' plan seems to have been introduced by Scots

St Patrick's Church of Ireland Cathedral in Armagh.

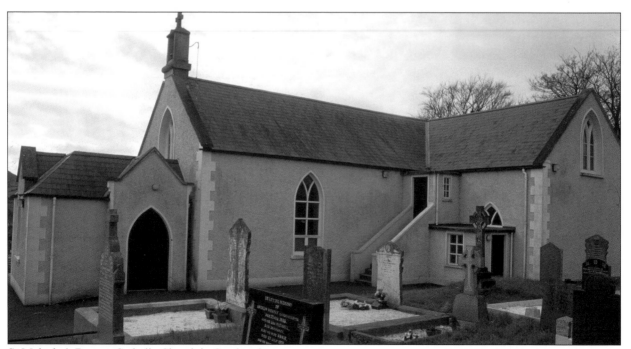

St Malachy's Roman Catholic Church in Camlough.

Presbyterians in the seventeenth century, but was also used extensively for early Mass houses. In the wake of emancipation, most of these early structures were demolished and replaced by more fashionable designs, so that this little building is now an extremely rare and valuable survivor, particularly with the external access to the galleries still intact.

The site commands wonderful views. It is only regrettable that the liturgical reordering of the sanctuary has resulted in such a total loss of coherence, with both the architectural elements of the building and the liturgical elements themselves. This, however, could easily be corrected and certainly does not challenge the historical importance of this architecturally modest building.

(See also colour section, page 19.)

CROSSMAGLEN
St Brigid's, Roman Catholic, Glasdrummon,

St Brigid's was built in 1928, under the architectural supervision of WH Byrne of Dublin, and was consecrated in 1932.

To see this church for the first time is an astonishing and unforgettable experience. Approaching up the narrow country road, one is totally unprepared to see a building of this size and architectural sophistication. Its history began with the demolition of Ravensdale Castle, one of Thomas Duff's last major works (1840) in the Lombardic style. Peter Sheerin bought the stones and presented them to the parish. Parts of the old building were reconstructed stone by stone – for example the portico and the campanile. It is reported that every stone was finally reused in this impressive new basilica. The re-ordering here has been sympathetic, with due respect to the fine architectural quali-

St Brigid's, Roman Catholic, Crossmaglen.

ty of the interiors.

(See also colour section, page 20.)

FORKHILL
Parish Church, Church of Ireland (former)

This was one of many rural churches funded by the Board of First Fruits in the 1790s. It became redundant through a combination of changing circumstances and population movement. Recently it has been skillfully converted, to designs by the architect Gerry Fay, to use as a private dwelling in a

The former Church of Ireland parish church in Forkhill.

St John's Church of Ireland, Kilcluney .

way that is totally reversible and without any structural alteration to the parent building.

KILCLUNEY
The Abbey at St John's, Church of Ireland

This surprising and unique construction dates from 1886. The architect and builder was the then rector, the Reverend Henry Hutchings.

There is nothing quite like the Abbey. The Reverend Hutchings had been strongly influenced by the Ecclesiologists and Tractarians. He wanted a ritualistic service, but many of his Calvinist-inclined parishioners were in opposition. Undeterred, he built a chapel of ease for himself, and by himself, in the grounds of the rectory. Here he conducted divine service as he believed it should be, in fellowship with those of his parish who agreed with him.

The Abbey recently came under threat because a new rectory was built and the old one put on the market. The enterprising parishioners of today recognised that the building should be saved, and made a plan to dismantle and rebuild it in the church grounds of St John's. This is where it stands now, disguised inside a modern masonry casing.

It is a little sad that this work of intense and sincere belief is no longer used for worship, but is instead part of a complex of halls and amenity facilities. At least it has been rescued and time may, one day, return it to its intended use.

The design is inspired by the twelfth century Romanesque style of Tuam Cathedral. In each bay on the ceiling are the achievements of the diocese of Ireland. Symbolism is abundant in the sanctuary screen, the roof decorations and the sanctuary itself.

The parish church of St John dates from 1794, It was financed by the Board of First Fruits with the encouragement of Archbishop Robinson, who was very keen to see the building of churches in the Armagh diocese and to put an end to worship in market houses and other secular buildings. The south aisle was added in 1864, to designs by Welland and Gillespie, architects to the Ecclesiastical Commissioners. This unassuming little building also contains other works of adornment by the Reverend Hutchings, which are instantly recognisable after the Abbey has been seen.

(See also colour section, page 20.)

KILLEVY
Old Churches

This is the site of one of Ireland's most important early Augustinian nunneries, founded by St Monenna (also known as St Bline) to whom the

Killevy Old Churches, Co Armagh.

Department of the Environment

holy wells, still revered, are dedicated. The site is recorded as having been plundered in 923 and suppressed in 1542.

There had been a round tower near the south-west corner of the church which is known to have fallen during the eighteenth century. The oldest church is to the west and developed its present form in the twelfth century.

Contiguous with it is the eastern church which is medieval, having a window in the decorated fifteenth-century style.

The former Friends' Meeting House in Lurgan.

Killevy was a large and wealthy parish, its clergy held in special esteem in the chapter of Armagh.

LURGAN
The Friends' Meeting House (former)

Built in 1880, this meeting house has now been converted for use as commercial offices, while a new structure has been erected on an adjoining site. The Friends were traditionally very numerous in the north of Ireland and their history is well documented in George Chapman's article (see bibliography) and FX McCorry's *Lurgan: An Irish Provincial Town 1610–1970*. The community grew fast during the settled period after the suppression of the 1641 Rebellion and the re-establishment of Lurgan as an important market and manufacturing town. This building represents a single phase in the history of the meeting houses here. Its recent replacement stands only a few yards away.

As on other sites developed by the Friends, the meeting house is part of a complex, including here a graveyard and a row of substantial town houses

MARKETHILL
Methodist

This three-bay hall is typical of the many such buildings erected by the Primitive Methodists around the 1800 period – unassuming and vernacular in character.

Most of these buildings have been superceded or

Markethill Methodist Church.

put to other uses or simply demolished, but here we have a rare and complete survivor.

NEWRY (see also Co Down)
St Brigid's, Roman Catholic

This modern church (designed by architects Smith and Fay) was built in 1968 to serve the new housing that was being developed in the Daisy Hill district of the town. Despite the innovative spirit of the time, the plan is a perfectly traditional 'T', with an aisled nave so wide that the seating is in four blocks across its width.

The construction is a concrete frame clad in natural materials. On the outside there is limestone in smooth ashlar blocks and on the inside is brick and natural timber. There is perimeter light from windows, but most of the light is from glazing near the ridge of the main pitch of the roof. The original fittings are specially designed to harmonise into a unified architectural experience. The building is a landmark, if a little forbidding from a distance. However, the interior is light, airy, spacious and welcoming.

St Colman's College Chapel, Roman Catholic

The chapel was built in 1937–38 and dedicated to Mary, Immaculate Mother of God. The architect was John J Robinson of Dublin.

This is a small and relatively insignificant building as seen from outside, yet the interior is a quite exceptional work of art. Every detail is specially fashioned to heighten an awareness of the sacred – using architectural language of proportion, texture, colour, lighting and symbolism. The design is intriguing and subtle, combining innovation and tradition, with the result that it is very difficult to put a label name on the style. It is somewhere between a stripped version of Romanesque and Art Deco. Of the fittings, the glass and decorative tile work are outstandingly beautiful, the work of Richard King in the studio of Harry Clarke.

The chapel is laid out on a basilica plan, with the entrance in the north wall at the west end. Over the

St Brigid's Roman Catholic Church, Daisy Hill, Newry.

entrance is a gallery, with beautifully curved projecting balustrades. Against the west wall are stalls for the bishop and his canons. Recently there have been changes in the sanctuary area – the resiting of the triumphal arch to the east wall (it had been built free-standing); and the pair of modern nave lights in the last bay before the sanctuary, break the rhythm of the overall design. However, both of these changes could easily be reversed.

(See also colour section, page 21.)

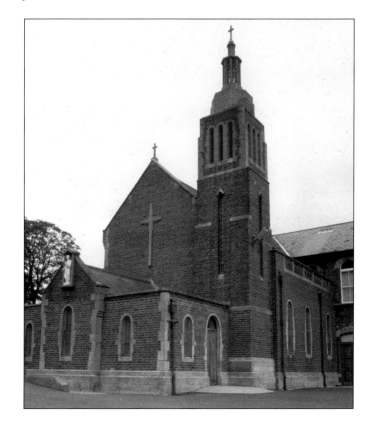

St Colman's Roman Catholic Chapel in Newry.

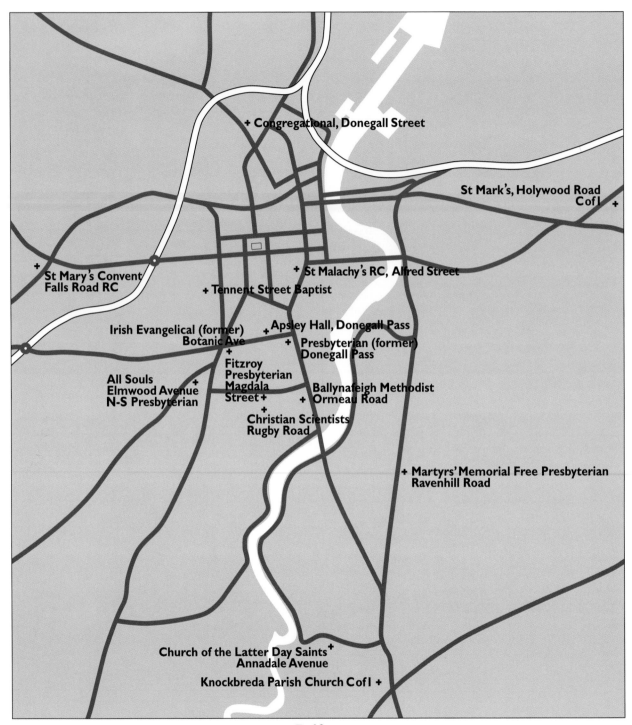

+ Congregational, Donegall Street

St Mark's, Holywood Road
C of I +

+ St Mary's Convent
Falls Road RC

+ St Malachy's RC, Alfred Street

+ Tennent Street Baptist

Irish Evangelical (former)
Botanic Ave
+ Apsley Hall, Donegall Pass
+ Presbyterian (former)
Donegall Pass

+
Fitzroy
Presbyterian
Magdala
Street +
All Souls
Elmwood Avenue +
N-S Presbyterian

Ballynafeigh Methodist
+ Ormeau Road

+
Christian Scientists
Rugby Road

+ Martyrs' Memorial Free Presbyterian
Ravenhill Road

Church of the Latter Day Saints +
Annadale Avenue

Knockbreda Parish Church C of I +

Belfast

Belfast

All Souls Non-Subscribing Presbyterian Church in Elmwood Avenue, Belfast.

All Souls Non-Subscribing Presbyterian, Elmwood Avenue

Here is an adventurous design as seen from several points of view. Dr Larmour writes that it is modelled on the fourteenth century Croyland Abbey in Lincolnshire. The church was constructed in 1895–96 and the architect was Walter Planck of London. The massing of solids in relation to voids is very subtle and looks forward in architectural time as well as backwards – there is far more to this design than just good copying. The plan form is unexpectedly episcopal. The congregation has published a short history, in which it states that the design reflects "the interest at the time on the part of the minister and congregation in establishing a more devotional type of worship". It is a unique and beautiful little building. (See colour section, page 22.)

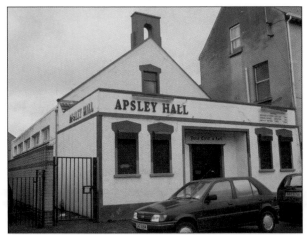

The unpretentious front of Apsley Hall in Donegall Pass.

Apsley Hall, Brethren, Donegall Pass

The hall at Currien, Florencecourt (see page 97), illustrates the simplicity of worship by the Brethren in a rural community. Apsley Hall confirms the same simplicity in an urban setting. Here, quite intentionally, there is absolutely no architectural pretension. All that is required of the building is shelter, yet this is as much a church as any of the other buildings included in this study.

Ballynafeigh Methodist, Ormeau Road

The congregation dates from 1838 and as a result of steady growth this, their third church, was built in 1897–99. The architectural firm in question was Forman and Aston. The foundation stone was laid by James Henderson, then Lord Mayor of Belfast.

The unconventional styling of the building is generally agreed to be influenced by contemporary North American architects like WR Emerson and is a Queen Anne Revival free style. The plan is more or less octagonal, which is a shape that Wesley himself is said to have favoured. The combination of the octagon with a gallery running around five of the sides brings a large number of people into close contact with the minister. It really is the model for a preaching church. The great pity is that, through time, the exterior has been stripped of so much of its original finery that it is now only a shadow of its original self.

Church of Jesus Christ of the Latter Day Saints, Annadale Avenue

The Church of the Latter Day Saints, or the Mormon Church as it is more popularly known, originates in the United States, and it is there, in the US headquarters, that the designs for their church buildings are prepared. This Belfast design is no exception.

The planning of the complex is reminiscent of rural Quaker meeting houses in its provision for

Ballynafeigh Methodist Church on the Ormeau Road, Belfast.

flexible use (see Grange, Co Tyrone, page 121). The main hall space is equipped with folding partitions so that it can serve a number of separate functions, as well as its primary function as a chapel. The essential elements for worship are housed in the bays nearest the main entrance. The building also provides for catering, instruction (with the provision of classrooms) and administration. Stylistically it is very much a building of its time – mid-twentieth century – with very few echoes from the past.

The Church of Jesus Christ of the Latter Day Saints in Annadale Avenue, Belfast.

Donegall Pass Presbyterian (former)

Made redundant by shifting population, this church was first converted to use as a joinery works and more recently as a warehouse. All the church fittings have been removed, but structural intervention has been minimal and is reversible.

Donegall Street Congregational

The present appearance of the church dates from building work in 1952, carried out under the supervision of architects Samuel Stevenson and Sons. The original church on the site was built in 1859–60, with additions in 1871. The rebuilding

The former Presbyterian Church in Donegall Pass, now used as a warehouse.

was necessitated by the extensive damage suffered during the World War Two blitz.

The style of the reconstruction is a free style perpendicular revival, well proportioned and with

Donegall Street Congregational Church in Belfast.

some imaginative detail. It makes a sympathetic composition with the older wing gables that frame it.

First Church of Christ the Scientist, Rugby Road

This is one of three churches in this study designed by a prominent British architect. There are a handful of other buildings in the province by Clough Williams Ellis, but this composition, built between 1922 and 1937, is the most monumental.

The church forms part of a pleasantly arranged complex, including the cloisters, the Sunday School, the caretaker's house and the Minor Hall. The style mixes Art Deco with Edwardian free style. The assured but subtle geometry of the group throw up a delightful play of light and shade. The interiors match up to the quality of the exterior. The church plan is traditional nonconformist: entering under a gallery, the opposite wall has a raised platform with twin reading desks and the seating is in three blocks with a double aisle. The furnishings are all contemporary and part of a unified overall design with the building itself. A strange feature is that the fine ornamental gates have no direct relationship with any of the entrances.

It is a pity that when the photographs were taken the external paintwork was in such poor condition, but by the time this description is in print this may well have been put to rights.

(See also colour section, page 22.)

A view of the Christian Scientist Church on Rugby Road, at the rear of Queen's University.

The meeting room in the First Church of Christ the Scientist on Rugby Road, Belfast.

Fitzroy Presbyterian, Magdala Street

This is one of a number of very episcopal-looking Presbyterian churches, in the Gothic Revival style, that sprang up in the expanding towns and cities of Ulster towards the end of the nineteenth century. The architects in question, Young and MacKenzie, designed quite a number of them, producing some very eye-catching and imaginative designs. This particular church was built between 1872 and 1874.

The exterior suggests a full blown cruciform and aisled Gothic interior, but in fact it is nothing of the sort. Instead you find a large single-span hall, architecturally more like a Tudor banqueting house than a medieval church. It is laid out on traditional meeting house lines, the pulpit having the dramatic backdrop of an elaborate organ case. Quite why the Gothic Revival became so popular with Presbyterians at this time is a little mysterious and deserves deeper study. (See also the First Presbyterian Church in Armagh, page 43.)

Irish Evangelical (former), Botanic Avenue

This former church is now 'The Empire' bar in one of Belfast's developing nightlife areas, close to Queen's University. This is another case where population migration has led to a church becoming redundant. The new use has been achieved at the expense

Fitzroy Presbyterian Church, Belfast.

Formerly the Irish Evangelical Church, now 'The Empire' bar, Botanic Avenue, Belfast.

of the church furnishings, but the structure has been retained without any serious alteration, either inside or out.

Knockbreda Parish Church, Church of Ireland

Knockbreda parish church, built in 1737, is the only church building in Ulster designed by the renowned Dublin architect Richard Castle (also Cassels). The apsed chancel, skillfully added in 1883 by Thomas Drew, reflects the strong Tractarian influence on the Church of Ireland at the time. The original expense of building had been met by the Dowager Viscountess Middleton.

The interior of 'The Empire' is still recognisable as a former place of worship.

There are not many classically-styled Anglican churches in Northern Ireland and most of those are early eighteenth century in date. Even this one has very few architectural details – the strongest and most uncompromising is the pedimented Gibsian

Knockbreda Church of Ireland parish church.

doorcase, below the tower. An unusual feature is the apsidal transepts.

Towards the end of the eighteenth century the graveyard at Knockbreda became a fashionable place to be laid to rest and as a result there is now a most interesting array of grave monuments.

Martyrs' Memorial, Free Presbyterian, Ravenhill Road

Designed by the architect Gordon McKnight, the format and furnishings of this modern building (1967–69) – while there is no attempt at stylistic revival – are firmly rooted in tradition. The pulpit is centrally placed on the long wall, and galleries on three sides bring a large number of people into close proximity to the preacher, all having a full

Martyrs' Memorial Free Presbyterian Church, Ravenhill Road, Belfast.

uninterrupted view of the pulpit. This arrangement is firmly focused on the preaching of the gospel. It is interesting to compare the plan of St Malachy's Roman Catholic church in Alfred Street (see below, page 60) where the same architectural format was used a century before. In this latter context, however, the focus is on the Sacraments and the altar.

A particular feature of the Martyrs' Memorial is the highly developed complex of support buildings, halls, offices, meeting rooms etc. This type of facility is becoming much more common.

An interior view of Martyrs' Memorial Free Presbyterian Church.

St Malachy's Roman Catholic Church, close to Belfast city centre.

St Malachy's, Roman Catholic, Alfred Street

The design of St Malachy's was chosen following a competition, with Thomas Jackson the successful architect. The church was constructed between 1840 and 1844, and there is no other church quite like it. The altar is on the long wall facing the main entrance and there are galleries on three sides. This form had been popular in pre-emancipation times, but the fashion had generally changed in favour of plans based on the long axis.

The late Gothic Revival style had also been used to great effect by the architect Thomas Duff,

in particular at Newry and Dundalk and his unexecuted design for the new cathedral in Armagh, but generally it does not seem to have been a favourite with Roman Catholic churchmen. However, at St Malachy's this style has been used to create a magnificent and very beautiful interior. The sanctuary has been remodelled twice – first in 1926 and again recently to provide for the conciliar Mass – but with very little damage being done to the architectural conception of the spaces. The interior makes an interesting comparison with the Martyrs' Memorial Church of a century later (above, page 59).

St Mark's, Church of Ireland, Holywood Road

This magnificent High Victorian composition in Ruskinian Gothic, while typical of the work of the architect, William Butterfield of London, is the only major and complete building designed by him in Ireland. The geometry is clear-cut and impressive, heightened in effect by the coloured stone banding. The tower is a major feature of the Belfast skyline. The plan is laid out on Tractarian lines, cruciform with an aisled nave. It is only in the chancel that there is any of the internal decoration for which other Butterfield churches are renowned. There is a very 'high' Anglican ring to the whole conception of the building.

The construction was in two phases – 1876–78 and 1889–91 – but it is all but impossible to see where the break was. The Ewart family were major benefactors and gave very generously towards the building. A beautiful addition is the electric corona-styled lights, specially designed by the architect Dykes Bower. Recently the building underwent a major overhaul and is now looking particularly resplendent.

An additional note of interest is that the author CS Lewis was baptised here.

(See also colour section, pages 23–4.)

An assured statement of High Victorian Gothic Revival architecture – St Mark's Church of Ireland on the Holywood Road.

St Mary's Dominican Convent Chapel, Roman Catholic, Falls Road

Here is the first major eccle-siastical work by Padraic Gregory, who was later to become the leading architect of his generation, working for the Roman Catholic Church across Northern Ireland.

The chapel, built in 1926–30, was an addition to the existing convent building of 1870 by John O'Neill. Designed in the Ruskinian Gothic Revival style, it was intended to serve the school as well as the Dominican sisters of the house. This being the case, an unusual plan was arrived at. This con-sisted of a great Gothic hall with a single north transept, the sisters provided for in a colle-giate format and the school in cross benches, both focused on the free-standing high altar. The altar was canopied by a majes-tic stone-built civory, set for-ward of the canted apse. Only the school transept is railed off from the altar. This carved stone railing is decorated with the emblems of Dominican martyrs.

The same attention to individ-ual detail is carried through the entire interior. The side altars to Our Lady and Thomas Aquinas are relatively low-key, so that the high altar is the undisputed focus from every point in the building. At the west end is a beautifully detailed musicians' gallery and, above it, the great rose window, with glass by

St Mary's Dominican Convent Chapel on the Falls Road.

Harry Clarke of Dublin. The acoustics of the building are marvellous – there is no need here for 'address systems'. The exterior of the building gives no clue to the treasures inside.

(See colour section, page 24.)

Tennent Street Baptist

This is one of a series of similar churches designed for the Baptists by the architect James A Hanna. The late Tudor Revival style is here influenced by the contemporary Edward-ian free style and the Arts and Crafts movement. It was built in 1904. Inside, the layout is fairly standard for nonconformist hall churches, and provides for the total immersion style of baptism. It is nicely detailed and well proportioned, with most of the original fittings and furnishings still in place.

The church activities have expanded greatly since the early days, so that now this little building is linked into a whole complex of ancillary halls and other amenity facilities.

(See also colour section, page 24.)

Tennent Street Baptist Church in Belfast.

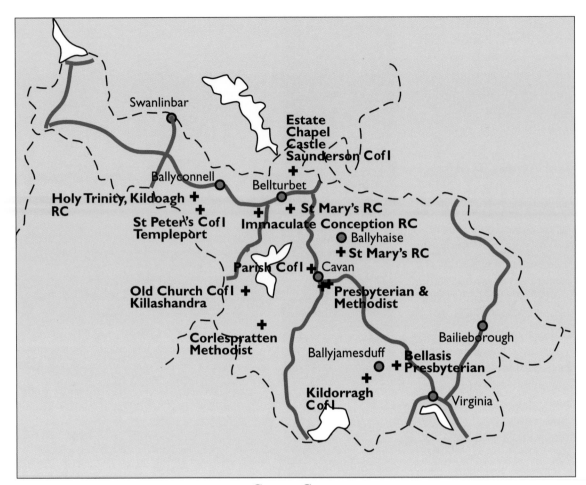

County Cavan

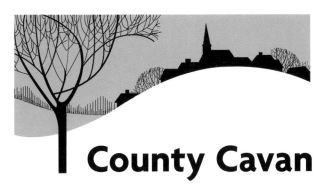

County Cavan

BALLYHAISE
Saint Mary the Virgin, Roman Catholic

Previous to its removal to its present site in 1942, this building served as the pro-cathedral to the Roman Catholic diocese of Kilmore. Then it stood in Cavan town, close to the road and in front of the present cathedral. In this earlier role it was dedicated to St Patrick. Kilmore was one of the last dioceses to get a new purpose-built cathedral, but however late it was in coming, the design by WH Byrne amply redressed that deficit.

Saint Mary the Virgin Roman Catholic Church in Ballyhaise, exterior (above) and interior (below).

The old building originated as a very simple pre-emancipation barn church. However, its present form and appearance relates, in the main, to the major renovations and extensions implemented over the period 1851–62. It was in these years that it was made fit for its cathedral role by means of the generosity of the congregation under the leadership of Bishop Browne, whose memorial is sited on the outside of the north wall. The form remains a seven-bay gabled hall, with simple Gothic detailing. The only irregularity is a large projecting porch midway along the south wall.

Further renovations in 1982 increased the seating capacity by incorporating the old sacristy into the body of the nave, but otherwise the work did little justice to this venerable chapel. The approach is by way of a sea of tarmac and the cathedral furnishings, which had been the crowning glory of the nineteenth century renovations, have been cleared away in their entirety.

BALLYJAMESDUFF
Kildorragh Church of Ireland

Built around 1880, Kildorragh church presents a charming, fully developed, ecclesiastical composition in miniature. The east end faces the public road, and from this direction the gables step in an inspired sequence from vestry to chancel to nave. At the west end the horizontal lines of the nave are foiled against the offset tower that doubles as an entrance and broaches in to support an elegant octagonal spire. Sadly, this exceptional little building is now redundant.

BELLASIS
Presbyterian

The history of the Bellasis congregation begins in 1826 when the Reverend King came to minister to local people who found it difficult to travel the distance to the meeting house in Ballyjamesduff. Problems arose over the first site selected for a new building, with the result that the completed works were dismantled and activities transferred to the present site.

When completed, in 1837, the church was a simple vernacular four-bay hall, originally orientated to a pulpit set centrally on the long back wall. The reordering was not implemented until 1961, when the present long axis arrangement was introduced and new pulpit furniture provided.

Against the south gable is a two storey, two roomed school, which was immediately nicknamed 'King's College' after the first minister. The curriculum, as in most Presbyterian schools of the time, was firmly based in the classics.

Kildorragh Church of Ireland, Ballyjamesduff.

Belasis Presbyterian Church.

St Mary's Roman Catholic Church in Belturbet (above) and the estate chapel at Castle Saunderson (below).

BELTURBET
St Mary's, Roman Catholic

St Mary's is one of a series of church building works inspired by Austin Quinn, Lord Bishop of Kilmore.

It was completed in 1957, just before the Vatican II Council changes began to take effect. The new building replaced an earlier chapel of 1835. The style is an economic Lombardo Romanesque. The form is a five-bay hall without interruptions, despite the expectation of a basilica plan, promoted by the triumphal, triple arch feature of the west front. Offset is an octagonal campanile rising from a square base.

(See also colour section, page 25.)

CASTLE SAUNDERSON
Estate Chapel

An estate chapel, built at the end of the nineteenth century, is a neat three-bay buttressed hall with a four-stage tower set axially against the west gable. The tower rises through the first three stages with a

The vault in the Castle Saunderson estate chapel.

square plan form, but for the fourth and last stage, now free-standing above the ridge of the main roof, it broaches into an octagon. The machicolated parapet provides the base for an octagonal stone spire. Detailing is eclectic, part Gothic and part Romanesque, but well composed.

The purpose was to combine as both a chapel of ease for the estate and as a mausoleum for the Saunderson family, many of whom are laid to rest in the crypt, while others, including Edward James Saunderson of parliamentary fame, are buried in individual graves amongst the trees.

The family is gone now and the demesne is run as a state forest. The building is no longer in use and is suffering from neglect.

CAVAN TOWN
Parish Church, Church of Ireland

This building was opened for worship in 1815, belonging to an era when many new churches were provided for urban parishes, helped by loans from the Board of First Fruits. John Bowden, to whom the design of this church is attributed, was chief architect to the Board. The Church of Ireland congregation and garrison in Cavan had previously used the nave of the pre-Reformation Franciscan friary. In many other towns secular buildings had been pressed into ecclesiastical use on the Sabbath, with the market house frequently meeting this need.

There is a presence about this building, sited on rising ground and planted around by ample broadleaf trees. The style is the usual Gothic of the time, vigorously crenelated and pinnacled. The design is axial and symmetrical. The progress of entry is a special experience: first into the cube of the porch; on through a three storey octagon within the tower, enhanced by a slender staircase serving two tiers of galleries and hung from wrought iron rods; then the rectangular cross passage of the narthex; and finally into the spacious well-lighted nave, broad and uncluttered by columns. The gallery fronts are decorated with Tudor roses and the ribs of the plastered ceiling spring from imposts enriched by beautiful little heads. The chancel and transepts appear to be additions and probably date from the 1860s, as does the refurnishing when the box pews and central aisle were replaced by bench pews, leaving only the side aisles. There are a number of memorials of quality around the walls, in particular to the Earl of Farnham of 1826.

(See also colour section, page 25.)

The Presbyterian and Methodist Churches

The Presbyterians built their church in 1834 and the Methodists completed theirs in 1874. Neither has any great architectural pretensions, but together they contribute positively to the local quality of the townscape. The special interest lies in the close grouping of these two buildings and their manses.

The Church of Ireland parish church in Cavan town.

The Presbyterian (left) and Methodist churches in Farnham Street, Cavan town.

This type of close grouping of nonconforming churches is repeated in other Ulster towns, for example Omagh and Newry.

CORLESPRATTEN Methodist

Here is a simple hall, nearly square, its only architectural pretension being the pointed Gothic windows. The form is typical of Methodist church buildings of the early nineteenth century and is a clear reflection of

Corlespratten Methodist Church and school, Co Cavan.

the self-reliance and enthusiasm of these congregations. Corlespratten congregation appears to have been a particularly lively one, inspiring a number of notable ministries over the years.

The building was erected in 1803 and suffered severe damage in the 'Big Wind' of 1839, losing its roof, a calamity repeated in 1903. These last repairs are recorded on the front wall and were supervised by Mr Elliott of Enniskillen. Mr Elliott's name crops up continually all across the west and south of Ulster, both in the context of the construction of new Methodist churches as well as in relation to programmes of maintenance and repair.

Grouped with the church is a school house which together, in the sheltering plantation of trees, appear as an oasis in an otherwise inhospitable landscape.

DRUMLANE
Church of the Immaculate Conception, Roman Catholic

With a datestone of 1846, this is a five-bay hall church, set on high ground roughly a mile west of Belturbet at Kilconny, above the road to Killashandra. The site is very bare, but it may once have been planted with trees. The applied detail is Gothic. Tall spikey finials crown the four corner buttresses and the figure of the Blessed Virgin crowns the west gable, protected by a cut stone cote. On the east gable above the sanctuary arch is a less ornate cote, housing the sanctus bell.

Inside, interest is focused at the two ends of the hall. At the west end is an elaborately detailed and arched gallery and at the east end the sanctuary is defined by a boldly modelled Gothic arch. Beyond is a rib-vaulted plaster ceiling and triple light east window.

KILLASHANDRA
The Old Church, Church of Ireland

Appropriately named, this building has a date stone recording the year 1688. The graveyard, which dates from the same year, is entered by an elegant pedestrian cutstone gateway and hosts a number of early memorials. The church building is a rectangular hall, now roofless, with a projecting entrance vestibule set midway along the long wall. The body of the church may have medieval origins; the detailed layout and furnishings can now only be surmised. A large part of the internal space is occupied by the mausoleum of the Martin family. The entrance vestibule is a curious brick barrel vaulted structure. On the left hand side is the doorway lead-

The Church of the Immaculate Conception in Drumlane.

The Old Church at Killashandra.

ing to the body of the church by way of a wide, stone-paved passage. On the right hand is a chamber reached by a flight of stone stairs and with a stone chimney flue. Set into the gable is the Southwell crest.

TEMPLEPORT
Holy Trinity, Roman Catholic (former), Kildoagh

Bearing a datestone for 1796, in its day this was one of the finest examples of a pre-emancipation barn chapel in Ulster. It was replaced in 1979 with the construction of a new church dedicated to St Mogue, a mile or so to the west in the townland of Kilsob. The old building still stands as a sad reminder of former days, degraded and forlorn. It is a six-bay narrow hall with entrances in bays two and

The former Holy Trinity Roman Catholic Church at Templeport.

five of the front wall. The altar once stood centrally against the back wall. The windows to the front are paired lancets with Gothic tracery, while gable windows lit the galleries.

The datestone of Holy Trinity Roman Catholic Church at Templeport.

St Peter's Church of Ireland, Templeport, Co Cavan.

St Peter's, Church of Ireland

This congregation had previously worshipped in the now ruined medieval church building on St Mogue's Holy Island in the centre of Templeport Lough. The new church was made possible by benefactions from local gentry that included the Blashfords, Finlays, and Johnstons, and was built around 1700. At this point in time the Established Church was very short of funds.

St Peter's has been altered on a number of occasions through its history. Towards the end of the nineteenth century the chancel was added and the furnishings replaced, but the earliest elements are likely to be the nave and vestry. Their juxtaposition suggest an original internal arrangement focused on a central pulpit. The tower and gallery date from around 1800. Of particular note is the very fine braced king post trussed roof frame. The wrought iron hangers, clasps and hand-made bolts suggest a mid eighteenth century date, but the girth of the timbers and the nature of the framing may be evidence that it was reassembled from much older material. There is glass by Heaton, Coulter and Blane of London and the Baroque, 1722, monument to the Blashfords is very fine. The graveyard is well tended and includes Roman Catholic graves.

(See also colour section, page 28.)

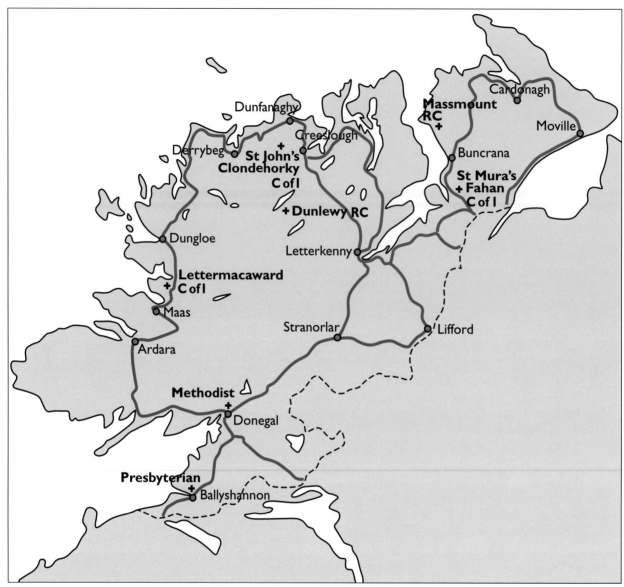

County Donegal

County Donegal

BALLYMORE
St John's, Church of Ireland, Clondehorky

This is an exceptionally elegant design by Michael Priestley, built in 1752, displaying unusually high levels of craftsmanship. The church is a four-bay hall, lighted through the south wall and by an immense venetian window over the Lord's table against the east wall. The bold rusticated gibsian cut stone dressings are characteristic of the late Baroque. There is a cut stone bellcote over the west gable, a projecting hipped porch, and a vestry added in 1853. Inside, the furnishings are typical of the 1750s. The ritualists of the late nineteenth century have left this church entirely alone. Although all is not original, it is all well matched. There is the usual western gallery for musicians, and one suspects that there would have been a more elaborate pulpit but it is difficult to be sure where this might have been sited. The driveway entrance, walled graveyard, and school house all help to compose a very attractive setting.

St John's Church of Ireland parish church in Clondehorky.

The interior of St John's, Clondehorky.

BALLYSHANNON
Presbyterian

Built around 1840, this is a fairly standard hall with rudimentary Gothic detailing, to which has been added a cross wing, creating together a 'T' plan. The extension is much more expressive than the original construction, with bold pinnacled corner buttresses, a stone bellcote in line with the ridge and unexpectedly large plate tracery windows, high up in each of the three new gables. These alterations and additions date from around 1885.

DONEGAL TOWN
Methodist

Built in 1858 in the Romanesque style favoured by the Methodist movement, this is a neat little hall, but here there are more embellishments and finer detailing than is usual. It is on a difficult but eye-catching site, against the abutments to Dr Joyce's Bridge. The river flows past one side so close that it has been known for fishermen casting their lines to break windows in the church with their weights. The interior has been carefully restored and the opportunity taken to make one or two practical changes. For example, a draft lobby has been formed by screening off the entrance below the gallery, but great care has been taken to maintain the Romanesque detailing in the associated join-

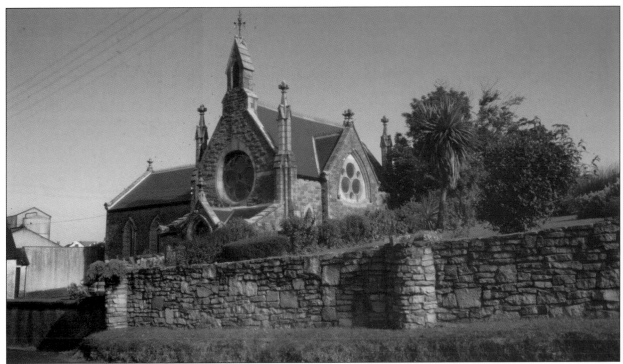

The expressive exterior of Ballyshannon Presbyterian Church.

ery details. The seating arrangements are the usual double aisle format, facing the holy table and reading desk, protected by a timber communion rail arcaded in Romanesque style. Below the church is a basement hall, separately accessed from outside. This is another common detail for Methodist churches of the period; Alistair Rowan notes that the same design appears at Ballymoney, Cookstown and Newtownards, although he has not been able to associate the design with any particular architect.

(See also colour section, page 29.)

DUNLEWY
Church of the Sacred Heart, Roman Catholic

Here we find a development of the Hiberno Romanesque, complete with round tower, built in 1877. Its design is similar to that of the Church of Ireland at Jordanstown (see page 40), built a decade earlier, both searching for a national identity in a changing political world. The form is not as elaborate as most of the architect Timothy Hevey's Gothic Revival designs. Outside there are buttresses only at

The Methodist Church in Donegal town.

the west end, where they stand as sentinels to the main door, and inside there is no arcading, just a simple open hall nave.

The bracketed, half-length colonnettes, that were very much his signature, decorate the apse of the sanctuary, marking it off from the nave. Outside, the rugged basalt walling is enlivened with polychrome bands of limestone and marble. However, much has been lost from the interior reordering. Hevey was renowned for his altar and furnishing designs, but sadly not a trace of his original work remains. Outside, reslating of the roof has failed to replicate the polychrome coursing of the original. Nevertheless, the building remains a dramatic eye-catcher on a particularly stunning site, with Errigal mountain as a backdrop.

The interior (left) and exterior (above) views of the Church of the Sacred Heart in Dunlewy.

The Church of Ireland in Fahan.

FAHAN
St Mura's, Church of Ireland

Built in 1820 to a design by John Bowden, the church at Fahan typifies those features most often associated with the rural parish churches of the Church of Ireland of the period: classical in proportion, Gothic in detail, and economic with ornament. The three-stage tower is crowned by four corner pinnacles and is set on the axis of the nave, the ground floor serving as an entrance porch. The nave is a simple hall of three bays. At the west end the elegant gallery is part of the original design, and at the east end the architect SP Close added the chancel in 1898. Concurrent with this addition, the whole church was refurnished. The east window depicts the Resurrection by Mayer and in the nave is a window by Evie Hone. The wall memorial to Elizabeth Jones is of historic and artistic value.

She was a close companion of Florence Nightingale. (See also colour section, page 29.)

LETTERMACAWARD
Church of Ireland

This is an early nineteenth century rendered hall church of three bays, financed by the Board of First Fruits. The design is simple and functional. The only architectural detailing is the Gothic tracery to the windows which are ranged down both sides, and a triple-light east window above the holy table. There is a cut stone bellcote over the west gable. The vestry is contemporary with the main building and there is a small gabled porch of the same vintage. The site is dramatic – the church nestles next to medieval ruins in its walled graveyard in an otherwise pitiless landscape.

(See also colour section, page 29.)

Lettermacaward Church of Ireland stands close to medieval ruins.

Massmount Roman Catholic Church, Rossnakil, overlooks Mulroy Bay.

ROSSNAKIL
Massmount, Roman Catholic

Massmount is a pre-emancipation chapel. It may be the building recorded as built by the Reverend Joseph Friel in 1785, but this is not certain. Its location is most striking – on a low cliff above the shore of Mulroy Bay. It is a lofty five-bay hall with a bellcote raised above the eaves line of the centre bay of the south wall. The walls are rendered and whitened and the windows are Gothic in form, but the character has more of the vernacular about it than any formal architectural style. The interior is reordered with some careful thought and attention to detail, harmonious with the intrinsic qualities of the parent building. The same careful hand may have been responsible for the new sacristy extension. The shape of the main building and the disposition of the windows would suggest the original arrangements had the sanctuary placed on the long wall, opposite the bellcote. The gallery arrangements may also have been altered – certainly some stray timber column sections have mysteriously found their way in amongst the present sanctuary furnishings.

The interior of Massmount Roman Catholic Church, Rossnakil.

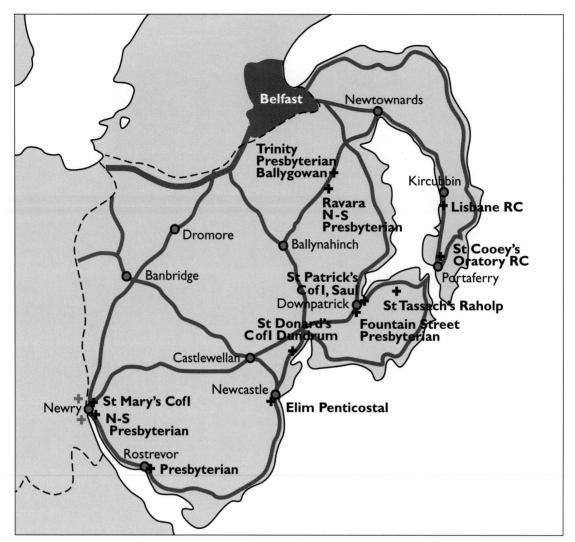

County Down

Note – grey crosses mark churches featured under Co Armagh.

County Down

BALLYGOWAN
Ravara Non-Subscribing Presbyterian

This church was built for a Unitarian congregation, which no doubt partly explains why the congregation in nearby Ballygowan found it necessary to display the fact that, by contrast, it stood for the Trinity.

This church, erected in 1837, is a perfect example of the intentionally plain, vernacular, hall-type rural meeting house, commonly built during the second half of the eighteenth century. The Non-Subscribing Presbyterian congregations have been most diligent in keeping their original buildings in use, rather than seeking replacements in the latest fashionable architectural style.

There is a stark, serene simplicity, careful attention to proportion, and relationship of solid to void that makes this a very appealing little structure.

Ravara Non-Subscribing Presbyterian Church in Ballygowan.

Trinity Presbyterian

Built at a time when Presbyterian churches were mostly designed in Classical Revival styles, it is interesting to find one that follows the earlier tradition of no outward show in the old meeting house vernacular mould. Such is the case with this church, built in 1838 for the Reverend J Gamble, the then minister.

It is also of interest to see the church named specifically 'Trinity', presumably in order that anyone considering joining the congregation should do so knowing quite clearly that Arian and Unitarian beliefs were not held here, as they were in nearby Ravara.

Inside, passing through the vestibule, is a hall, more or less square, with a continuous gallery supported on slender iron columns sweeping around three sides. It is beautifully furnished with the best timber that the Empire could provide, finely joinered and producing a sense of solidity and well-being.

Added to the rear of the church is an extensive hall complex for social activities, opened on 22 October 1994. This type of facility is becoming an ever more common feature of church life.

DOWNPATRICK
Fountain Street Presbyterian

The congregation in Downpatrick was founded around 1660. The first meeting house on this site was built in 1826 and served the military garrison in the barracks nearby, at the top of Scotch Street.

The present church, built in 1954–55 to the designs of architects Ferguson and McIlveen, is of conservative design based on the traditional 'T' plan, just as the much older Stream Street church of 1710 had been. The practicality of this form is amply proved in this neat and airy building. The only feature that is in any way unusual is the furnishings for the minister, where in this case the communion table is placed centrally, with the pulpit or reading desk off-set to the left. This may have come about because of the depth of the minister's dais front to back. (See also First Presbyterian Church, Strabane, Co Tyrone, page 126.)

Trinity Presbyterian Church, Ballygowan.

Fountain Street Presbyterian Church in Downpatrick.

DUNDRUM
St Donard's, Church of Ireland

The construction of St Donard's (1886) was financed by the Marquis of Downshire who was, at the time, promoting Dundrum as a spa, port and bathing place.

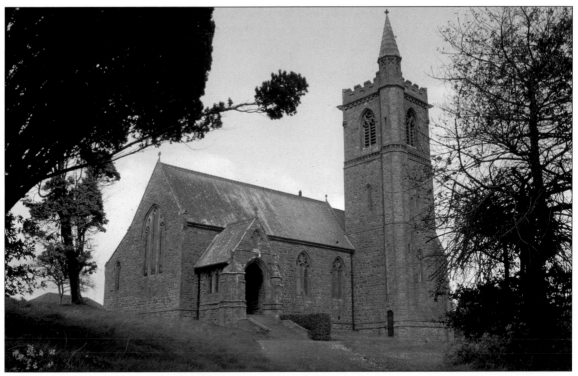

Two views (above and below) of the impressive St Donard's Church of Ireland, Dundrum.

The architect in question, Sir Thomas Drew, was the son of a Church of Ireland clergyman and designed a considerable number of churches for that denomination, most of these in the Gothic Revival style. His ecclesiastical masterpiece, however, is St Anne's Cathedral, Belfast, when he chose Romanesque.

At Dundrum, some subtle geometry, the choice of stones and the form and landscaping of the site, as designed by George Maitland, all add up to a very pleasing and impressive composition. The orientation, north-east/south-west, makes the best of the site. There is an open entrance porch at the southeast corner of the nave and the vestry is behind the organ, at the base of the tower. The internal arrangements are on ecclesiological lines, with a precessional nave, north aisle, and baptistry at its west end.

KIRCUBBIN
Roman Catholic Chapel, Lisbane

There were never many pre-emancipation Mass houses in the north of Ireland, and most of those have been replaced in post-emancipation times. This chapel, built around 1777 for Father Daniel O'Doran, parish priest of Ardkeen, is a very rare survivor. A quick glance at the outside of this building does not immediately reveal the denomination that it serves. All Christians were building vernacular halls of this type at this time. An interesting feature of the materials used in its construction are the local Tullycavy slates. These too were commonly used in the Ards, until cheap transport in the mid nineteenth century brought imported slates at a price against which

Two views that capture the simplicity of Lisbane Roman Catholic Church in the Ards peninsula.

which the local product could not compete.

On entering, note the holy water stoop outside, set in against the door jamb. Inside, the box pews are set on to a stone-paved floor in two ranks, each side of a central aisle. The sanctuary is raised on a simple wooden platform and demarcated by a rudimentary wooden communion rail that is interrupted at the south end by a single confessional. This too is an early piece of furniture, with the penitent placed outside and only the priest enclosed. The rear compartment of the same framework is the sacristy, but there is no special entry door for the priest from the outside. The sanctuary has not been reordered in any way – even the corona candelabra is a contemporary fitting. Where else would you find such a perfect reflection of simple devotion?

This is a most remarkable survivor and long may it be cherished.

The large stone cross in the graveyard bears the following inscription:

beneath this cross erected to their memory, pray for the souls of the Rev. John McGuire our esteemed P.P., Walter Kehoe our devoted C.C. and Rev. James Linney P.P. of Loughguile. Their bodies lie beneath the spot where stood the old altar, on which they offered Mass for their flock many of whom now . . . [next line ineligible] . . . May their souls rest in peace.

Elim Pentecostal Church in Newcastle functioned previously as a lifeboat house.

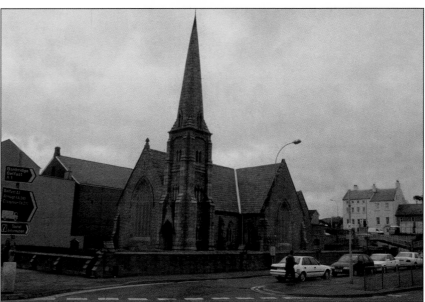

The Non-Subscribing Presbyterian Church in Newry stands close to the main roundabout with exits to Dublin, Warrenpoint and Belfast.

NEWCASTLE
Elim Pentecostal, Downs Road

Not all building conversions in relation to religion are of churches to other uses. Here, the old lifeboat house has been successfully put to a new use by the Pentecostal Church. The building dates from 1880, designed in the Arts and Crafts style, then in the very front line of architectural fashion.

NEWRY (see also Co Armagh)
Non-Subscribing Presbyterian, John Mitchel Place

This church was originally built for the Unitarian (Arian) congregation in the town in 1852–53. It was the first major work by the Newry-born architect WJ Barre, after he had set up his own practice in the town. It may also be the first cruciform, Gothic

St Mary's Church of Ireland, Newry.

Revival design for any nonconformist congregation anywhere in Ireland. Somehow the church looks much larger than it in fact is, but this deception is corrected if you view the building in direct relationship to St Mary's, just a little further down the street.

St Mary's, Church of Ireland, John Mitchel Place

As the town of Newry spread down from the higher ground above Water Street, where the settlement had been founded, into the newly filled ground behind the stone quays of the expanding port, the original St Patrick's church became less convenient for its parishioners. It was therefore decided to build a new church, more accessible to the developing middle class suburbs. The work commenced in 1810 and was completed nine years later.

The result was an elegant architectural composition in the Gothic style, integrated into the town planning of the area – a landmark at the entrance to the port as it had developed at that time. The architect responsible was Patrick O'Farrell.

The exterior is impressive and the interior lives up to expectations. The entrance is by way of a restricted passage, below the tower, from which you emerge into a spacious and well-lighted galleried arena. The proportion and emphasis of this space was altered when, in 1886, the chancel was added by Thomas Drew in the Gothic Revival style and the furnishing reordered to follow Tractarian Catholic principles. It is of interest to compare the detailing in these two sections of the building, both of which are good examples of their own type. The orientation is said to be due to the fact that the ground to the west was not fit to carry the weight of the tower.

Many of the fine wall monuments were resited from St Patrick's on the hill above.

(See also colour section, page 26.)

PORTAFERRY
St Cooey's Oratory, Roman Catholic

Here is an interesting and imaginative design where the plan is asymmetric and makes a play from inter-relating curves. This creates a gently graded crescendo of natural light within, reaching its greatest intensity in the sanctuary. However, this architectural excitement is not so apparent in the vertical dimension. The work of the great French architect of this century, Le Corbusier, has had some influence here. The church was built in 1966–68, with McLean and Forte as architects.

The contrast with the character of the surroundings is still remarkable, even after the lapse of 30 years.

RAHOLP
St Tassach's

This is said to be the church of Bishop Tassach who, as Muirchu accounts, administered the Viaticum to the dying St Patrick, thus making it one of the earliest ecclesiastical buildings in the whole of Ireland.

New and old – St Cooey's Roman Catholic Church in Portaferry (above), and the ruins of St Tassach's at Raholp (below, *Department of the Environment*).

A document of 1210 records Bishop Malachy as giving the church building to the Abbot of St Patrick's in Down. It is again recorded in the papal taxation roles of 1306. In the visitation records of 1622 it is recorded as a ruin. In 1915 Francis Joseph Bigger instigated basic restoration work and photographs were taken by WA Green before work began. It was restored again by the Historic Monuments Branch of the Department of the Environment only a few years ago and is now in state care.

The structure is a simple stone-built rectangle, with no architectural decoration or features. There are doorways in the west and south walls and a narrow east window. The north wall had collapsed before any surviving record was made. This type

Rostrevor Presbyterian Church.

and form of church building seems to have been the norm for several centuries in Ireland.

ROSTREVOR
Presbyterian

Built in 1850–51 to provide for local families and members of the local military garrison, the new church replaced Mary Street Dispensory which had been used for meetings over the preceding five years. Despite an unremarkable exterior in a simplified Gothic Revival style, the interi-

or is beautiful and unspoilt. The entrance is under the gallery and the furnishings of the church are laid out on the long axis, with box pews arranged symmetrically on either side of a single central aisle. This is a most unusual arrangement for a Presbyterian meeting house. The roof structure is exposed and there is a complete set of early bracket lamps.

At the back of the gallery are two painted panels displaying the Ten Commandments. Panels of this sort used to be commonplace in most Protestant

One of Ulster's most famous and most beautiful churches – St Patrick's Church of Ireland, Saul.

churches, but are now quite rare. They originally have been sited to either side of the pulpit. I am told they were obtained from the Church of Ireland in Rostrevor.

SAUL
St Patrick's, Church of Ireland

This building was erected in 1932–33 to commemorate the 1,500th anniversary of St Patrick's landing as a missionary in Ireland. The architect was Henry Seaver. The style is Hiberno Romanesque, and the structure consists of a hall church with shallow chancel and round tower that provides a vestry at ground level and a belfry above.

This is a very old Christian site. Edward Bruce destroyed the abbey then standing in 1316. Legend has it that this was the site of the barn originally given by Dichu to St Patrick for his use, when he landed in AD 462. There are certainly medieval remains within the graveyard. The small roofed cells may be graves over which chapels or chantries have been built, where Masses for the dead could be said.

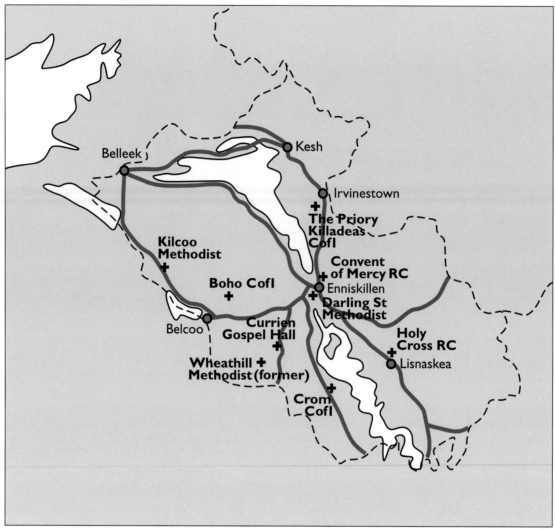

County Fermanagh

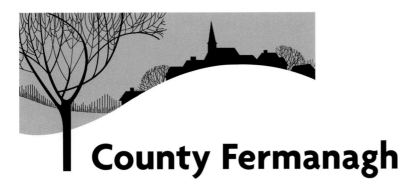

County Fermanagh

BOHO
Church of Ireland

Boho parish church was originally built in 1777 and restored around 1830. It is a very simple three-bay hall, with a lobbied entrance under the tower and a small vestry outshot on the north wall. The structure incorporates a medieval doorcase in the west wall, brought from the pre-Reformation site to the north of the present building.

The seating, with the holy table against the east wall providing for ministration from the north side, follows Calvinist practice.

The railing of the sanctuary is of the simplest form and is likely to be original. Some re-organisation of furnishings has taken place at the east end to provide for a choir, and it is likely that the pulpit was once positioned centrally, in front of the holy table. This arrangement was quite common until the middle of the nineteenth century. The font remains in its traditional place, close to the west entrance.

It is interesting to note the very close similarities, in form and furnishings, with the Methodist church at Kilcoo, only a few miles away. (See page 99 for Kilcoo Methodist Church, and the colour section, page 26, for a further photograph of Boho.)

Boho Church of Ireland, Co Fermanagh.

CROM
Parish Church, Church of Ireland

Crom parish church was built in 1840–44 and the architect is likely to have been JS Mulvany. The tower was added as a memorial to Selina, Countess of Erne, and dates from 1885; the architect for this addition being William Fullerton.

The building is an estate church, that is to say it was built by a landlord, in this case the Crighton family, for their tenants and themselves. It stands on an isolated site near the shores of Lough Erne; the majority of its congregation have traditionally reached it by boat. The furnishings included a fam-

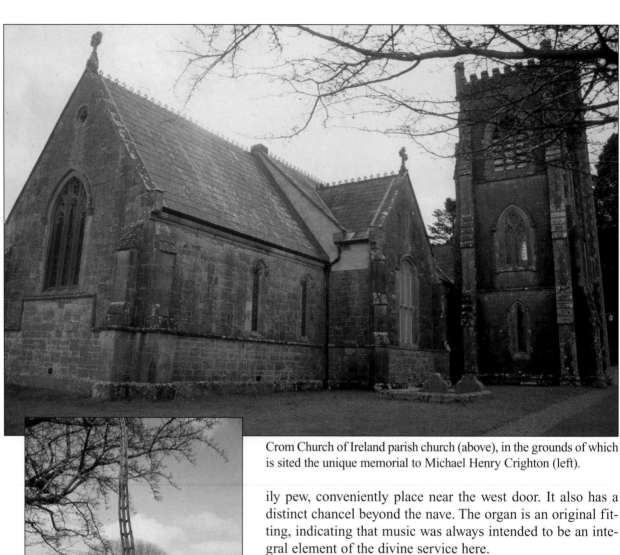

Crom Church of Ireland parish church (above), in the grounds of which is sited the unique memorial to Michael Henry Crighton (left).

ily pew, conveniently place near the west door. It also has a distinct chancel beyond the nave. The organ is an original fitting, indicating that music was always intended to be an integral element of the divine service here.

In the churchyard is the very remarkable memorial to Michael Henry Crighton who died in 1970.

ENNISKILLEN
Chapel of The Convent of Mercy, Roman Catholic

This building, dating from 1904 and designed by the architect William Scott, has a hall plan of extreme simplicity. However, this has not prevented the creation of a building which, both inside and out, has dignity, repose and beauty. It borrows nothing from the earlier adjacent convent buildings, and yet its novel design creates no conflict with its neighbours. It is full of innovation and at the same time deeply conservative. It skillfully projects ancient Catholic forms into the twentieth century, without any distortion. The style combines

One of Enniskillen's landmark buildings – the Chapel of The Convent of Mercy, exterior (above) and interior (below).

Hiberno Romanesque, Byzantine and the Arts and Crafts. It owes a great deal to the epoch-making chapel for University College Dublin, created by the hard work of John Henry Newman half a century before. This line of architectural development had been stopped in its tracks by the overwhelming tide of the Gothic Revival and did not develop and become acceptable in Ireland until the 1930s.

The arrangement is collegiate, with fitted stalls along the walls of the nave. The sanctuary is housed in a pro-

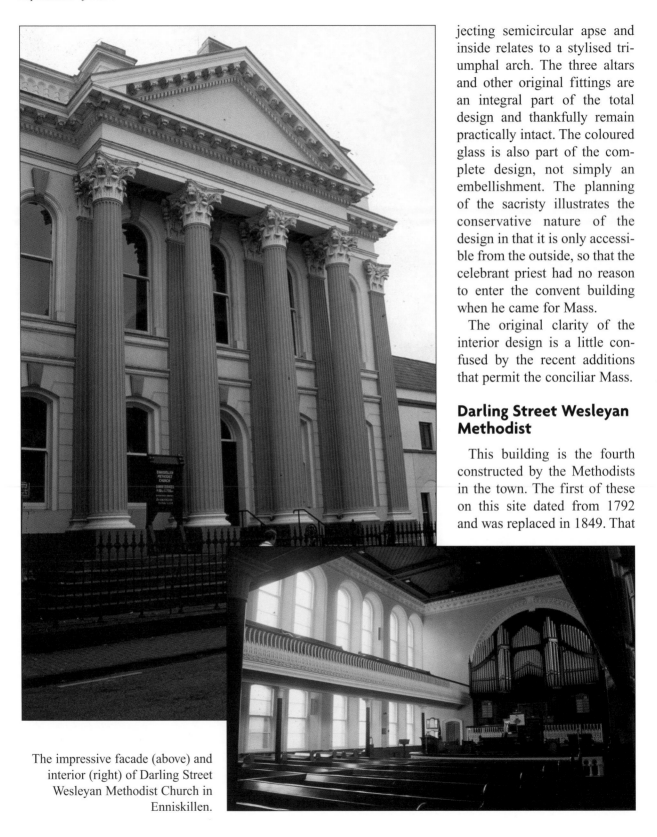

jecting semicircular apse and inside relates to a stylised triumphal arch. The three altars and other original fittings are an integral part of the total design and thankfully remain practically intact. The coloured glass is also part of the complete design, not simply an embellishment. The planning of the sacristy illustrates the conservative nature of the design in that it is only accessible from the outside, so that the celebrant priest had no reason to enter the convent building when he came for Mass.

The original clarity of the interior design is a little confused by the recent additions that permit the conciliar Mass.

Darling Street Wesleyan Methodist

This building is the fourth constructed by the Methodists in the town. The first of these on this site dated from 1792 and was replaced in 1849. That

The impressive facade (above) and interior (right) of Darling Street Wesleyan Methodist Church in Enniskillen.

structure survived until 1888 when the present McArthur Hall was constructed. The new Darling Street church was built in 1865.

The street presentation of this building is full scale classical Roman Corinthian. Inside the design is High Victorian. The architect, WJ Barre, was a native of Newry and his other works included several Methodist churches (see also the church in Moy, page 125). Barre also designed for the Presbyterians (see Newry, page 87), the Church of Ireland (see St Anne's, Dungannon, page 121) and the Roman Catholic Church. One of his most prestigious designs, however, was for the Ulster Hall, and it is with this building that the Enniskillen church has most affinity, particularly in the predominance of the organ case.

The furnishings are distinctly nonconformist, reflected particularly in the seating plan, with a double aisle non-precessional arrangement and the architectural dominance of the preaching desk (the Word) over the table (the Sacraments). Some of these features may date from the refitting of the interior by the architect Thomas Elliott in 1883.

FLORENCECOURT
Currien Gospel Hall

The congregation here was founded in 1890. This particular structure dates from 1961, replacing an earlier hall. It is characteristic of many buildings erected by the Christian Brethren since their foundation in Ireland by Edward Cronin around 1830.

Two views of Currien Gospel Hall in Florencecourt.

The building is functional and unadorned. The two foci, the Word and the Sacrament, are accommodated – the Word against the gable wall and the Sacrament at the centre. The arrangement, whether intentional or not, is reminiscent of a synagogue plan, with central bimah and the ark for the scrolls against the gable. The limited participation of the women of the congregation has similar echoes. This must be placed in the context that segregation of men from women was also the custom with other denominations until fairly recent times.

(See also Apsley Hall, Belfast, page 54.)

The Methodist Church in Wheathill, Florencecourt (above and below), was converted for private use in 1984.

Wheathilll Methodist (former)

The architect is not recorded in any of the major reference books, but the same design, with variations, was used for a number of small meeting houses in the area. It seems reasonable to conjecture that the same local architect, Thomas Elliott, who designed the McArthur Hall of 1888 in Darling Street, Enniskillen, also designed this building. Wheathill church was built around 1885.

It is a simple, hall-type

Kilcoo Methodist Church in Garrison.

meeting house, distinguished by a well-proportioned, picturesque version of the Romanesque Revival style. It is beautifully constructed of dressed, squared rubble stonework.

The church became redundant as congregation numbers dropped and in 1984 it was most carefully converted to use as a private dwelling. The work included an extension which has faithfully copied the architectural features and materials used in the original building. Even though the floor area has been more than doubled, the form of the design subtly maintains the original church building as the dominant element of the new grouping.

GARRISON
Kilcoo Methodist Church

This church was built in 1890 on land given by John Owens, who had previously made a barn available for meetings. Construction was by voluntary labour and the architect was again Thomas Elliott. Kilcoo church was constructed at the end of a period of growth in the Methodist movement, particularly in Co Fermanagh, where a great many small meetings developed.

The building is a simple three-bay hall and a double cube in volume. The entrance is at one end and the reading desk at the other. The bench seat behind the reading desk is an unusual feature. The seating is arranged on each side of a central aisle.

The Priory Church of Ireland in Killadeas (above), in the grounds of which stands a well-known relic of early Christian Ireland – the carved Bishop's Stone (left).

It is interesting to compare the similarity of its form and features to that of the nearby Anglican church at Boho.

KILLADEAS
The Priory Church, Church of Ireland, Rockfield

Built in 1864 and probably designed by W Armstrong, this is an estate church for the Irvine family. The tower is dated 1881. The Priory is constructed on the ancient site of the Yellow Church of the Culdees, part of which was still standing in 1825. From this early Christian period in Ireland there remain several carved stones in the graveyard, the most remarkable of which is the Bishops' Stone, depicting a coped Bishop carrying a crozier and bell.

The plan is cruciform, with at one end a defined sanctuary and chancel and at the other a shallow projecting babtistry. Set into the return against the chancel and the south transept is the bell tower. Inside, the fittings appear to be original and some beautifully encaustic tiled pavements have been incorporated. The Gothic Revival style is evident throughout the exterior and interior.

(See also colour section, page 26.)

LISNASKEA
Holy Cross, Roman Catholic

Holy Cross was built between 1902 and 1907, the architect TF McNamara using a Gothic Revival style, drawn from French models. The plan is basilica in form, with an apsidal sanctuary. The building is quite late in date for this approach. By this time the Hiberno Romanesque was generally the favoured style for new Roman Catholic churches.

Holy Cross Roman Catholic Church in Lisnaskea.

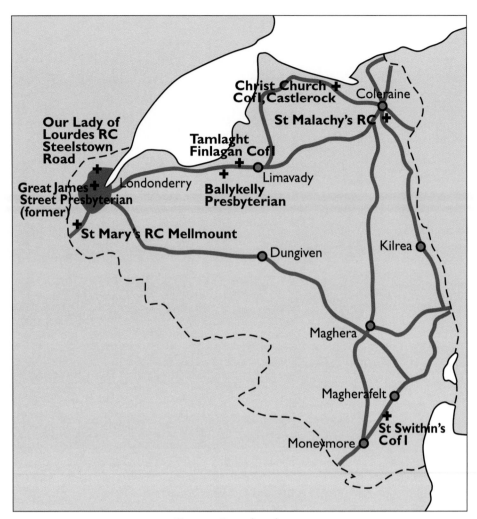

County Londonderry

County Londonderry

BALLYKELLY
Presbyterian

Built in 1827 and financed by the Fishmongers' Company of London, Ballykelly Presbyterian church was designed by the architect Richard Suitor.

This is a very large church. The style is at the frontier between the vernacular and formal architecture, but it is classical proportions and rudimentary classical details that win the day. The strong geometry of the building, together with its size, provide a very powerful message.

The interior is planned on the long axis, with the entrance in the north gable and the pulpit at the opposite end against the south wall. This arrangement was gradually taking the place of the emphasis on the long wall and the auditorium-type plans, as seen at Randalstown (see page 39).

The Presbyterians across the country were vigorously promoting education, and the classical styles in architecture paralleled the classical education pursued in their academies.

Tamlaght Finlagan Parish Church, Church of Ireland

This parish church was built in 1795 for Frederick Augustus Hervey, Earl Bishop of Derry, by his architect Michael Shanahan. The chancel was added in 1851 and the north aisle in 1859 by Joseph Welland, architect to the Ecclesiastical Commissioners.

The style is Gothic, much favoured by the Church of Ireland at the time. The careful proportions and fine decoration of the tower and spire make this

Ballykelly Presbyterian Church.

Tamlaght Finlagan Church of Ireland.

Christ Church in Castlerock.

church stand out as one of the very best of its type. The subsequent development of its plan clearly reflects the liturgical reforms within the Anglican Church that took place during the nineteenth century. These works, including the restoration of 1934, have all been very sympathetic to the original architectural con-conception. The building makes an interesting comparison with that in Upper Ballinderry, built a generation later.

Like so many churches, its setting includes a plantation of trees – an important element in its charm.

CASTLEROCK
Christ Church, Church of Ireland

Christ Church, built in 1868–70, is cruciform in plan and quite small, with the entrance under the tower at the west end of the north wall. The style is a simple Gothic Revival, the design carried out by the architect Frederick William Porter for the Clothworkers' Company of London. The proportions are a little strange and the relationship of the spire to the tower is uncomfortable, but inside is a different experience altogether.

The arrangements in-corporate the more ritualistic forms that followed from the Oxford Tractarian influences. The architect's skilful planning has allowed the vestry and organ to become an integral part of the total design. The walls are lined in red hand-made brick and the fittings are exquisitely designed to create a harmonious, intimate architectural experience. Of particular note are the brass candelabra set in two lines down the nave – those in the sanctuary are a little more elaborate. A fine corona light is hung centrally. The stained glass is also of good quality and the colours harmonise with the architecture.

The church seems to be very much as built, with no obvious alterations, either inside or out.

(See also colour section, page 27.)

COLERAINE
St Malachy's, Roman Catholic

St Malachy's was built in 1935–37 to designs by Padriac Gregory. The style is a type of stripped Romanesque and the plan is essentially a basilica, but interrupted by the tower halfway down the south aisle. This intrusion has allowed a Lady Chapel to be subtly created and has also provided for a processional way from the sacristy. The rose window in the west wall shows, in its

Exterior and interior views of St Malachy's Roman Catholic Church, Coleraine.

glazing pattern, a particular interest that Gregory had in this feature, repeating it again and again in other church designs, but always with great innovation in the detail of the glazing subdivisions – no two are the same.

The architect's own personal piety reads strongly in his architectural creations. The recent reordering of the sanctuary has kept most of the elements of the original design, but in rearranging them has confused their original coherence. There is also something desolate and unloved about the landscape in which the building is set.

(See also the Dominican Convent on the Falls Road in Belfast, page 62.)

DRAPERSTOWN
Presbyterian

Although the form is simple and austere, this building is quite definitely classical in proportion and the entrance front displays a distinct pediment and shallow pilasters. It is therefore a link between the vernacular character of the early Presbyterian meeting houses and the architecturally-styled churches of the later nineteenth century.

The present Draperstown church was planned and built by the Drapers' Company of London. Work began on the construction in 1827 and was completed around 1840. The architect was most likely to have been WJ Booth.

LONDONDERRY CITY
Great James Street Presbyterian (former)

Architect Stewart Gordon designed this church (built in 1835–37) for the third Presbyterian congregation in the city. It became known as the Scots' Church. The interior was redesigned in 1863 by Boyd and Batt.

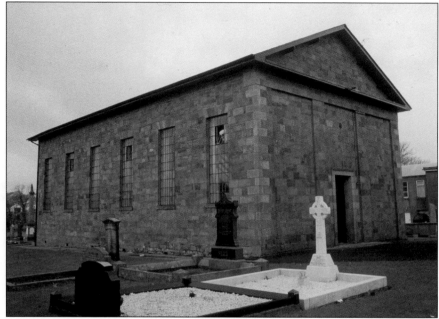

A building of substance – the Presbyterian Church in Draperstown.

The portico steps to the former Great James Street Presbyterian Church in Londonderry.

Great James Street church, combined with the manse, is a very important feature of the townscape of this late Georgian city suburb. The Greek Revival style reflects the Presbyterians' thirst for learning and scholarship, that had led to the founding of important classical academies, the most famous of which is the Royal Belfast Academical Institution. The most remarkable feature of this particular design is the massive, scrolled, ramped stops to the portico steps.

Sadly, this church was made redundant and is now only partly used by a glass studio. The fabric is beginning to show distinct signs of neglect.

The ultra-modern design of Our Lady of Lourdes Roman Catholic Church in Londonderry has provoked both admiration and condemnation.

Our Lady of Lourdes, Roman Catholic, Steelstown Road

This uncompromisingly 'modern' design, built in 1975, was the work of the architect Liam McCormick. In 1978 the RIBA award assessors commented that the building "immediately expresses the designer's intention to produce a simple and dignified place of worship" – while Alistair Rowan describes it as "a slate-hung tent stepped in three stages with a bivouac porch offset at the end"! McCormick developed his individual approach to church design throughout the 1970s, becoming acknowledged as the leading exponent in Ireland of modern church design. No two of his buildings are the same, but all share an exciting interplay of clear uncluttered geometrical forms.

The plan form and furnishings here relate to the liturgy of the Vatican II Council, but it is not a church in the round. There is a strong east-west processional axis and the three-staged roof holds shadowy reminders of the ancient division into nave, chancel and sanctuary. The landscaping around the chapel is a positive and integral part of the overall design.

(See also St Brigid's, Newry, page 50, and St Cooey's Oratory, Portaferry, page 89.)

MAGHERAFELT
St Swithin's, Church of Ireland

The architect Joseph Welland was commissioned directly by the Salters' Company of London to design this church, completed in 1856–58. The company headquarters are in St Swithin's Lane in that city and this is the origin of the dedication in Magherafelt.

This was one of Welland's largest church designs and replaced an earlier more modest building, the remains of which stand in the nearby graveyard.

The design is cruciform and symmetrical in all its major features. The western tower is axially

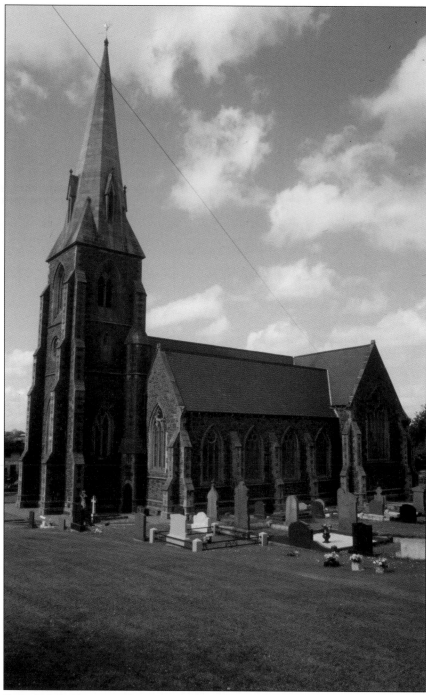

St Swithin's Church of Ireland in Magherafelt.

placed, but it is not the entrance, as one might have expected. Instead, the space below the tower provides for a baptistry and the main door is into the north aisle. Because of the unusual width of the building, the roof is three parallel double pitches, with internal valleys over the arcades. This arrangement prevents lighting from a clerestory and so the architect has introduced an ingenious decorative dormer light over the nave. The distinct chancel is part of the original design and the ordering and furnishings thoughout are characteristic of a time when ritual was reintroduced into Church of Ireland worship. The architectural style is Welland's favoured English, early decorated Gothic, and characteristically the elegant framing of the roof is exposed to view.

(See also colour section, page 27.)

St Mary Mellmount, Roman Catholic

This is an uncompromising rectangular structure, designed by Patrick Haughey and completed in 1970, the upper half and roof clad in copper fronting. The church is set in an equally uncompromising sea of tarmac. The architectural composition includes a school and parochial house of matching style and materials. There is landscaping and planting, but its environmental effect is limited. Inside, a single unrelieved space is lighted from continuous clerestory windows. Opposite the main entrance the sanctuary is set on the long wall from which a fan of aisles separate groups of seating and radiate to an ambulatory around the outer walls. The inspiration for the liturgical arrangements is the New Mass of the Vatican II Council.

Another modern design – seen on this occasion from the inside – St Mary Mellmount Roman Catholic Church.

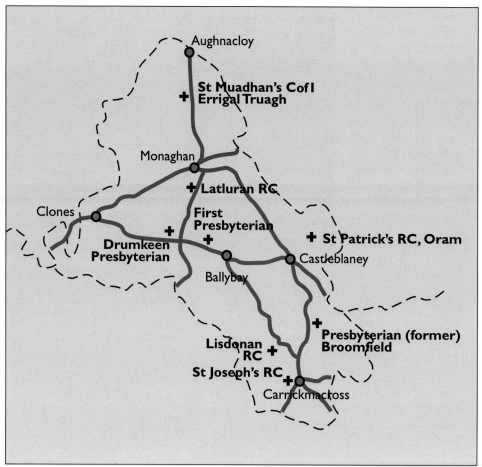

County Monaghan

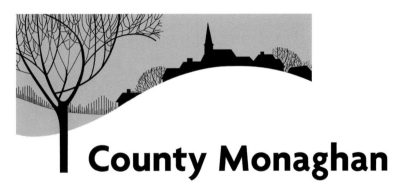

County Monaghan

The First Presbyterian Church in Ballybay.

BALLYBAY
First Presbyterian

This is a barn church of six bays, built in 1786, and constructed in rubble stone with cut stone dressings and a half hipped gabled roof. The siting is one mile outside the town, reflecting Penal Law restrictions on dissenting congregations. This particular congregation was formed in 1697, but no records survive of their buildings prior to the present one, the construction of which is well recorded. Members of the congregation took an active part in the building work and, because of the chronic shortage of home-grown timber, all structural members had to be imported through Newry.

Much of the original fabric survives. The door set in the east gable is original, together with the freestone, Gibsian-styled casing to the opening. The glass in the fanlight and the other windows all twinkle with the irregularities so characteristic of old crown glass.

The interior was reordered in 1888–89, as were many other Presbyterian churches at that time, when the pulpit was moved from the long wall to create a new orientation along the length of the building. In the original format it is recorded that the congregation were permitted to construct their own seating, an arrangement that led to some irregularity and disorder. The old pulpit was reused with only minor modifications.

In the church grounds is a school building dating from 1836, and on an adjoining site the seceding congregation built the 'Ballibay New Erection', very similar in form and massing to the mother house.

Broomfield Presbyterian Church (above and below) has now been converted, with IFI funding, for the use of a local community group.

BROOMFIELD
Presbyterian (former)

Another example of the reuse of a redundant church building is to be found in the case of Broomfield Presbyterian church, built in 1841. In this instance a local community group has been supported by the International Fund for Ireland in the creation of new accommodation, providing for a meeting/exhibition room, offices and catering and toilet facilities. The architects involved in this project were ABC and Associates of Dundalk. The conversion of churches is always problematic and is bound to create conflicts. Here the major community area, with its galleries, maintains a comfortable, spatial relationship with the original elements and creates a welcoming, well lit, convenient and adjustable space. The same care has gone into the curtilage works. Hopefully similar care will continue to influence signage and management of the building in the future.

Lisdonan Roman Catholic Church in Carrickmacross (above) and its datestone (below).

CARRICKMACROSS
Lisdonan Roman Catholic Church

Built in 1812, according to its datestone, Lisdonan is a five-bay hall pre-emancipation chapel. Since Maurice Craig's recorded visit in 1974, there has been a drastic reordering of the interior. At least the sanctuary is still centred on the back wall, but so much else has been lost!

Outside, the historic presence is still strong. There are two entrances, to keep the men and women separate, and the free-standing iron bell frame is evocative of the penal days, when there was prohibition of bell ringing by all but the Established Church.

The rocky graveyard tells its own story.

(See also colour section, page 30.)

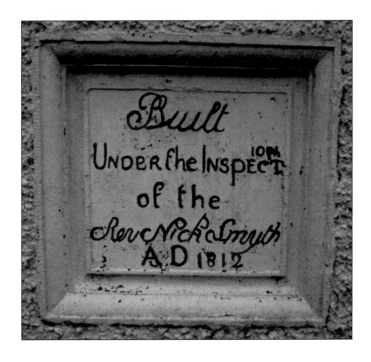

The imposing structure that is St Joseph's Roman Catholic Church in Carrickmacross.

St Joseph's, Roman Catholic

This building, constructed between 1861 and 1888, is of cathedral-like proportions. It was conceived in the architect JJ McCarthy's favoured thirteenth century French Gothic style and modelled in Pugin's footsteps, on a firmly ecclesiological format.

Beyond the loggia is an arched nave of four bays to the crossing. The transepts are close to the east end, with the sanctuary occupying the single bay beyond.

The massing of the architectural elements is more complex than is usual in McCarthy's church designs. The composition builds through a hierarchy of elements to triumph in a single offset stone spire of great elegance.

A reordering of the sanctuary has been achieved without serious conflict with the original architectural conception of the interior. In the aisle windows the wonderful coloured glass, from Harry Clarke's studio, is quite exceptional.

(See also colour section, page 30.)

DRUMKEEN Presbyterian

Drumkeen is a narrow gabled, vernacular, rural barn-type church, with a contiguous school house against the upper gable. The group is all rendered, windows are paired lancets and the gables have dressed stone copings. The site catches the eye, set, as it is, on rising ground above the road. The inscription over the main door records works to the building in 1828 and 1889. The original year of construction was 1803.

The entrance is via a loggia below a gallery. Once inside, the furnishings are set out in the twin-aisled arrangement common to most Presbyterian churches. The pulpit is dated 1855 and set in front of it is the holy table. There is no choir box.

A memorial of note is to Sir Thomas Crawford, Honorary Surgeon to Queen Victoria, who died in 1895.

The plan form of the school is one classroom over another. To segregate the boys from the girls, the upper classroom was made accessible only from the front of the building, while the lower could only be accessed from the back.

MONAGHAN TOWN
Latlurcan, Roman Catholic (former)

It is difficult to visualise that this modest pre-emanci-

Exterior and interior views of the Presbyterian Church in Drumkeen.

pation chapel, built around 1790, in fact served as pro-cathedral to the diocese of Clogher right up to the consecration in 1892 of JJ McCarthy's new cathedral that now towers above it on the hill.

It has a simple gabled barn format of three bays. The windows have semicircular heads and interlaced Gothic glazing. The layout suggests that the

altar was set on the long wall, but none of the furnishings survived.

The building now stands forlorn and neglected in a sea of grave monuments, redundant, no longer even in use as a mortuary chapel, as it had been for many years. It would be better to create a controlled ruin than to let it slowly fall apart.

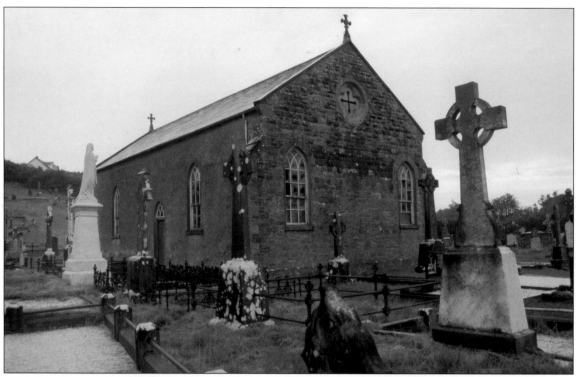

The Latlurcan Old Church (Roman Catholic) in Monaghan town (above), and St Muadhan's Church of Ireland, Errigal Truagh (below).

MULLINACROSS
St Muadhan's, Church of Ireland, Errigal Truagh

Built in 1834 with a loan from the Board of First Fruits, the present building replaced a medieval church, the remains of which can be seen in the old graveyard, a short distance to the west. Across the road is the holy well of St Muadhan (or St Mellan). Parish records begin in 1442; in 1659 Sir Toby Caulfield received grant of the parish; and by 1834 the local proprietor was Lord Rathdonnell. Other landed families having connections with the church include the Anketells and Singletons.

The architectural features are limited to the paired Gothic lancet windows and some finely dressed stonework, in particular the gable pinnacles and bellcote that have a striking elegance. The form of the building is simplicity itself. The nave is a three-bay hall, the roof supported by cast iron trusses representative of the Church of Ireland's early interest in this material. The chancel projection appears to be of contemporary construction, making it one of the earliest churches to have this arrangement.

The church, glebe house, medieval ruins and the holy well are unified by a common landscape and planting, which also seem to date from the 1830s.

(See also colour section, page 31.)

ORAM
St Patrick's, Roman Catholic

A 'T'-planned, pre-emancipation chapel, constructed around 1800, St Patrick's is one of the few to survive the post-famine replacement building programmes. Here is a simple traditional building, very expressive of its time.

Even more rare is the remarkable completeness of the interior. The sanctuary furnishings are practically intact. The new altar table has been subtly designed and stands on stone piers, open underneath so that it represents the least possible visual barrier to the appreciation of the old altar beyond. There is a reverence here and a strong unity between the elements, often lacking in the reordering of churches today.

St Patrick's Roman Catholic Church in Oram (both pictures) dates back to around 1800.

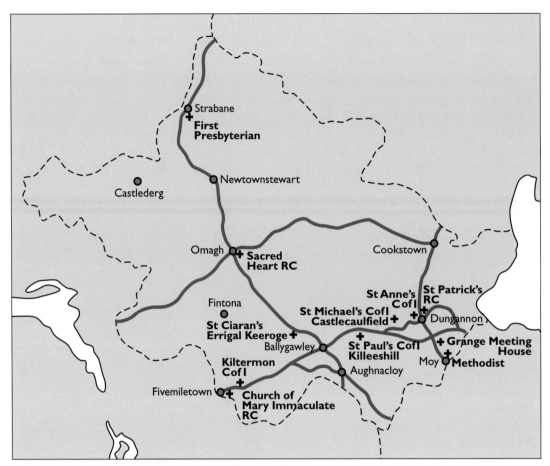

County Tyrone

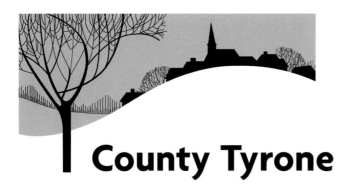

County Tyrone

An aerial view of St Ciaran's ruins, Errigal Keeroge, near Ballygawley.   *Department of the Environment*

BALLYGAWLEY
St Ciaran's, Errigal Keeroge

This striking, prominent site has one of the longest Christian pedigrees of any in the county. Originally on this site there was a monastery associated with St Ciaran. The remains of a round tower was recorded as recently as 1810 and there is a high cross of similar date, which appears never to have been completed. Across the road is a holy well. The next phase of building was probably associated with the 1489 founding of a Franciscan monastery, which building also served as a parish church in medieval times. The layout of the site is well illustrated in the aerial view.

CASTLECAULFIELD
St Michael's, Church of Ireland

Built during the 1680s, St Michael's replaced the earlier church, sited at Donaghmore, which had been destroyed in the 1641 Rebellion. The change of site was most probably due to the influence of Lord Charlemont. Some dressed stonework was brought from Donaghmore, including the late Gothic traceried window, now in the south wall of the nave. The whole east end of the church, including transepts, chancel and vestry, was added in 1860. In 1909 the nave arcades were removed, creating a single uninterrupted space. As part of the same works, unrecorded texts painted on the walls, probably the

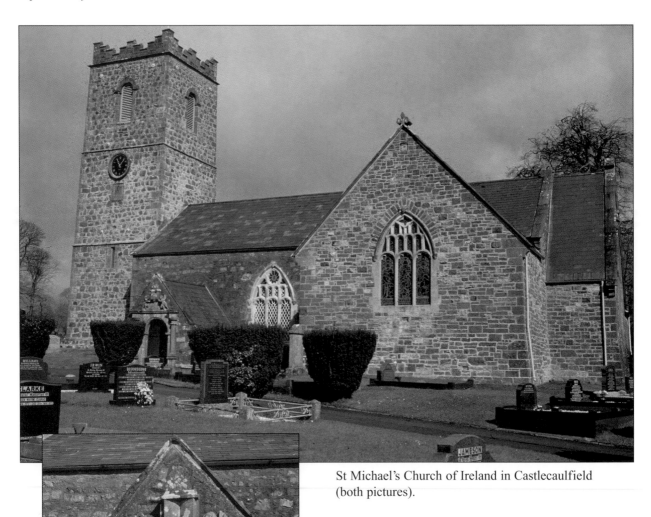

St Michael's Church of Ireland in Castlecaulfield (both pictures).

Commandments, were painted over. Some medieval carved stones are built into the fabric, including a sundial dated 1485.

Other features of interest include the charming vernacular rendering of classical architectural forms in the dressings to the south and west doorways; also the mobile pulpit, said to have been made for the Reverend George Walker who died at the Battle of the Boyne. Mobile pulpits used to be common Anglican church furniture, but this is the only one I know of to have survived in Ulster. It used to have legs, but these were cut off in 1891 for the use of the worshipful master of the local Orange lodge. Inside and outside, in the graveyard, there are a considerable number of memorials of interest and beauty. This site is a particularly fine store of historical interest.

A photograph that captures the peaceful rural simplicity of the Friends' Meeting House in Dungannon.

DUNGANNON
Friends' Meeting House, Grange

The earliest surviving building in this complex dates from 1756, but there had been a meeting at Grange at least as early as 1653. The group of buildings, as they now stand, date from 1816.

The large meeting house is the newest building in the group. This divides into three compartments or can be used altogether as one. This building is directly ahead as one enters the gates into the gravelled forecourt. To the right is the old meeting house and behind, under the same roof, the caretaker's lodging, and beyond that, the stables. Detached, just beyond the stables, is a coach house. The presence of a coach house and stables reflects the wide area served, with meetings held periodically bringing Friends from further afield. Behind the buildings is the graveyard which is landscaped with trees and lawns. There is even a toilet block to the left (south) of the main meeting house that must be of a similar age, ie early nineteenth century.

There is no elaboration here or formal architecture, but rather a wonderful tranquillity. Yet this is not achieved by accident and although there must

An interior view of the Friends' Meeting House in Dungannon.

never have been a master plan for the site, the common purpose has fashioned a place of beauty in the sight of God.

St Anne's Parish Church, Church of Ireland

This structure, completed in 1865, replaced an earlier church. Its asymmetrical plan shape and the liturgical reversal, ie the chancel at the west end, is probably the result of the irregular shape of the site.

St Anne's Church of Ireland in Dungannon (both pictures) is a fine example the the High Victorian Gothic Revival style.

The style is High Victorian Gothic Revival and is generally agreed to be the masterpiece of the architect WJ Barre.

The arrangements are ritualistic and there is an air of mystery, quite unlike his Methodist church in Enniskillen (see page 96), which is four square and unambiguous. It is a very impressive building both inside and out, of cathedral-like proportions. It was completed shortly before disestablishment.

The furnishings are also of a high quality, harmonising with the building, but not designed by the architect himself.

St Patrick's, Roman Catholic

The style of this building, erected between 1867 and 1889, is High Victorian Gothic Revival, based on a basilica plan, and out of many church designs this is one of the architect JJ McCarthy's most ambitious. The Irish hierarchy strongly favoured this form of architecture. Who knows what impact a different choice of style might have had on the total outlook of Roman Catholicism in Ireland. This could be the subject for another book, but not this one.

This design makes an interesting comparison with St Anne's by WJ Barre, just up

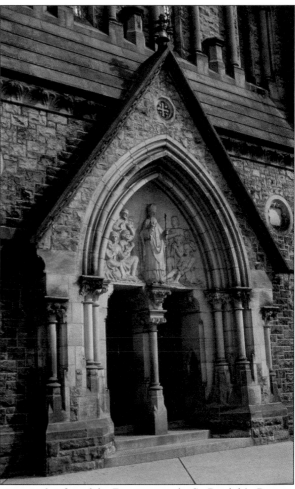

Another example of High Victorian Gothic Revival architecture to be found in Dungannon is St Patrick's Roman Catholic Church (above, left and right).

the road and also illustrated here. The interior fittings are mostly the work of the architect's son, CJ McCarthy; all have a very clear harmony based on French originals of the thirteenth century.

(See also colour section, page 31.)

St Paul's, Church of Ireland, Killeeshill

The present building dates from 1768 and the transepts were added in 1861 by Welland and Gillespie. The history of the site, however, is much older, with the first written record in the papal taxation register of 1302. The record of clergy goes back to 1407.

A notable landmark from the A4, heading west, is St Paul's Church of Ireland, Killeeshill.

There are many interesting grave stones and the graveyard is still used by Roman Catholics as well as Anglicans. It is said that the church was used by both denominations until the Roman Catholic chapel was built locally. This practice seems to have been quite common as the Penal Laws were relaxed, leading up to emancipation.

To the south an avenue connects with the Glebe House, which is now in private ownership. The square squat tower, with Gibsian doorway, is contemporary with the nave. Most of the furnishings seem to have been replaced when the transepts were added, although some of the chancel fittings may be older. The original building was a fairly typical hall church of the time. Extension by adding transepts is unusual – more commonly an aisle was built. From a distance one could easily be deceived into thinking the nave and tower were the additions and the original had the communion table on the long wall.

A closer view of St Paul's Church of Ireland, Killeeshill.

The Church of Mary Immaculate in Fivemiletown.

FIVEMILETOWN
The Church of Mary Immaculate, Roman Catholic

This church was built around 1871 and financed to a significant degree by the local landlords, the Montgomery family. The design is High Victorian, with a very definite Mediterranean feel about it. The open arcaded loggia is an unusual feature for the north of Ireland, while the use of coloured tiles on the external walls of the west end enlivens the whole aspect. The interior does not quite live up to the promises made by the outward appearance; nevertheless, while it is a modest building it has great individual character. Could it be the work of Alexander McAlister?

Kiltermon Chapel of Ease, Church of Ireland

This church, dating from 1820, illustrates the Church of Ireland at its most basic. It comprises a hall of five bays – with the holy table against the east wall – a projecting draft lobby porch and a small vestry outshot. The only pretence at any architectural style is the pyramid shaped pinnacles, the bell cote and the Gothic windows, with decorative cast iron lights. Its sheer simplicity is very striking.

MOY
Methodist

This is a solid practical church, designed in a simplified Romanesque style and built in 1861 at the

Kiltermon Church of Ireland.

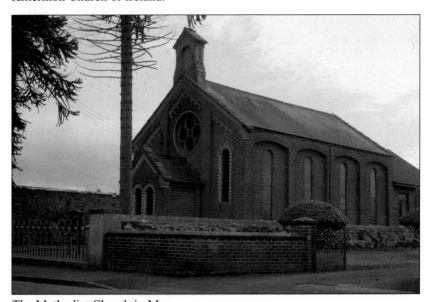

The Methodist Church in Moy.

time of the great Methodist Revival. The congregation predates the building by many years and had previously met in a series of other buildings in the town. The architect, WJ Barre, was engaged to design quite a number of other Methodist churches about this time, including the large classical church in Enniskillen, also illustrated in this book. Barre was favoured by Lord Charlemont, for whom he designed a major remodelling of Roxborough Castle (now demolished). The site of the church was originally part of the Charlemont estate.

There is an interesting little memorial inside the church to the Methodist preacher John Smith, beaten to death by a mob in 1774 because of his beliefs.

The Church of the Sacred Heart – an umistakeable feature of the Omagh skyline.

OMAGH
Church of the Sacred Heart, Roman Catholic

This design came towards the end of the career of the architect William Hague Jnr. It could be argued that he should be marked in this book by work from his native County Cavan, but this Omagh church, built between 1893 and 1899, is a culmination of his amazing catalogue of completed ecclesiastical designs and his continuous championship of the Gothic Revival style.

The west work is the crowning glory of the composition. The flanking towers of differing heights have inspired many legends and myths, but there is no doubt at all that this arrangement is intentional. Otherwise, the external treatment is bland and uninspired. However, the interior lives up to every expectation. The plan is laid out to a basilica form and shares the French Gothic style of the west front. The exposed timber framing of the nave breaks at the double scale chancel arch to give a special definition to the sanctuary.

(See also colour section, page 32.)

STRABANE
First Presbyterian

The congregation here is an old one, having been founded in 1659. The present meeting house is on the site of the old manse and replaced the building of 1871 which was destroyed by fire in 1938. The deign was by Thomas Houston and the work was completed in 1955.

It is a light, airy, brick-built hall, with detailed cast concrete dressings and impressive chunky offset bell tower. The interior is simple, clean and uncluttered, approached through a glazed vestibule below a gallery. The layout is unexpectedly episcopalian, with a central aisle flanked by seating set at an angle and on a gently sloping floor. The pulpit is offset to the left, while seating for the elders and the communion table occupy a recess not unlike a chancel and lighted by a good quality coloured glass window – "Christ and the little Children" designed by Morris and Co. The finely executed joinery sets the tone. To the right is an angled feature for the choir, breaking symmetry, and expressed outside in the shape of the minor hall behind it.

(See also colour section, page 31.)

A church of modern appearance, reflecting its relatively recent construction (1955) – First Presbyterian Church, Strabane.

Bibliography

Articles

Chapman, GR, 'Quaker Meeting Places in the Lurgan area in the 17th Century', *Review: Journal of the Craigavon Historical Society*, Vol 2, No1, 1972

Larmour, Paul, 'Profiles of Ulster Architects', *Perspective Magazine*, 1994–98

Radford, Raleah, 'The Earliest Irish Churches' (Oliver Davies lecture, 1977), *Ulster Journal of Archaeology*, Vol 40, 1977

Turner, Harold W, 'From Temple to Meeting House', *Religion and Society 16*, 1979

Books

Aalen, FHA, *Atlas of the Irish Rural Landscape*, Cork University Press, 1997

Acheson, Alan, *A History of the Church of Ireland 1691–1996*, Columba Press, 1997

Breakey, JC, *Presbyterian Church Architecture in Ireland*, np, 1966

de Brettny, Brian and Mott, George, *The Churches and Abbeys of Ireland*, Thames and Hudson, 1976

Brett, CEB, *Buildings of County Antrim*, UAHS and Ulster Historical Foundation, 1996

Craig, Maurice (unpublished), Second Preliminary Survey of Buildings of Historic and Artistic Interest in Cavan, 1974

— (unpublished), Second Preliminary Survey of Buildings of Historic and Artistic Interest in Monaghan, 1974

Curl, James Stevens, *Classical Churches in Ulster*, UAHS, 1980

Gallogly, Daniel, *The Diocese of Kilmore 1800–1950*, Killenm Mitchell, O'Fraem, 2000

Historic Monuments of Northern Ireland, DoE NI, 1983

Hamlin, Ann, *The Early Church in County Down to the 12th Century, Down History and Society*, Geography Publications, 1997

Hughes, Kathleen and Hamlin, Ann, *The Modern Traveller to the Early Irish Church*, Four Courts Press, 1977

Larmour, Paul, *Belfast: An Illustrated Architectural Guide*, Friars Bush, 1987

— *The Arts and Crafts Movement in Ireland*, Friars Bush, 1992

Leask, HG, *Irish Churches and Monastic Buildings*, Dundalk, 1955

Nesbitt, David, *Full Circle: A Story of Ballybay Presbyterians*, Cahans Publications, 1999

O'Laverty, JO, *Diocese of Down and Connor; Ancient and Modern*, Davidson, 1980

Richardson, Norman, *A Tapestry of Beliefs: Christian Traditions in Northern Ireland*, Blackstaff Press, 1998

Rowan, Alistair, *Buildings of Ireland: North West Ulster*, Penguin

Sheehy, Jeanne, *JJ McCarthy and the Gothic Revival in Ireland*, UAHS, 1977

Turner, W Harold, *From Temple to Meeting House*, Morton, 1979

UAHS Buildings series

Whone, Herbert, *Church, Monastery, Cathedral; An Illustrated Guide to Christian Symbolism*, Element Books, 1977

Index

Italics indicates an illustration of, or relating to, the subject matter.